LAYERS of REALITY

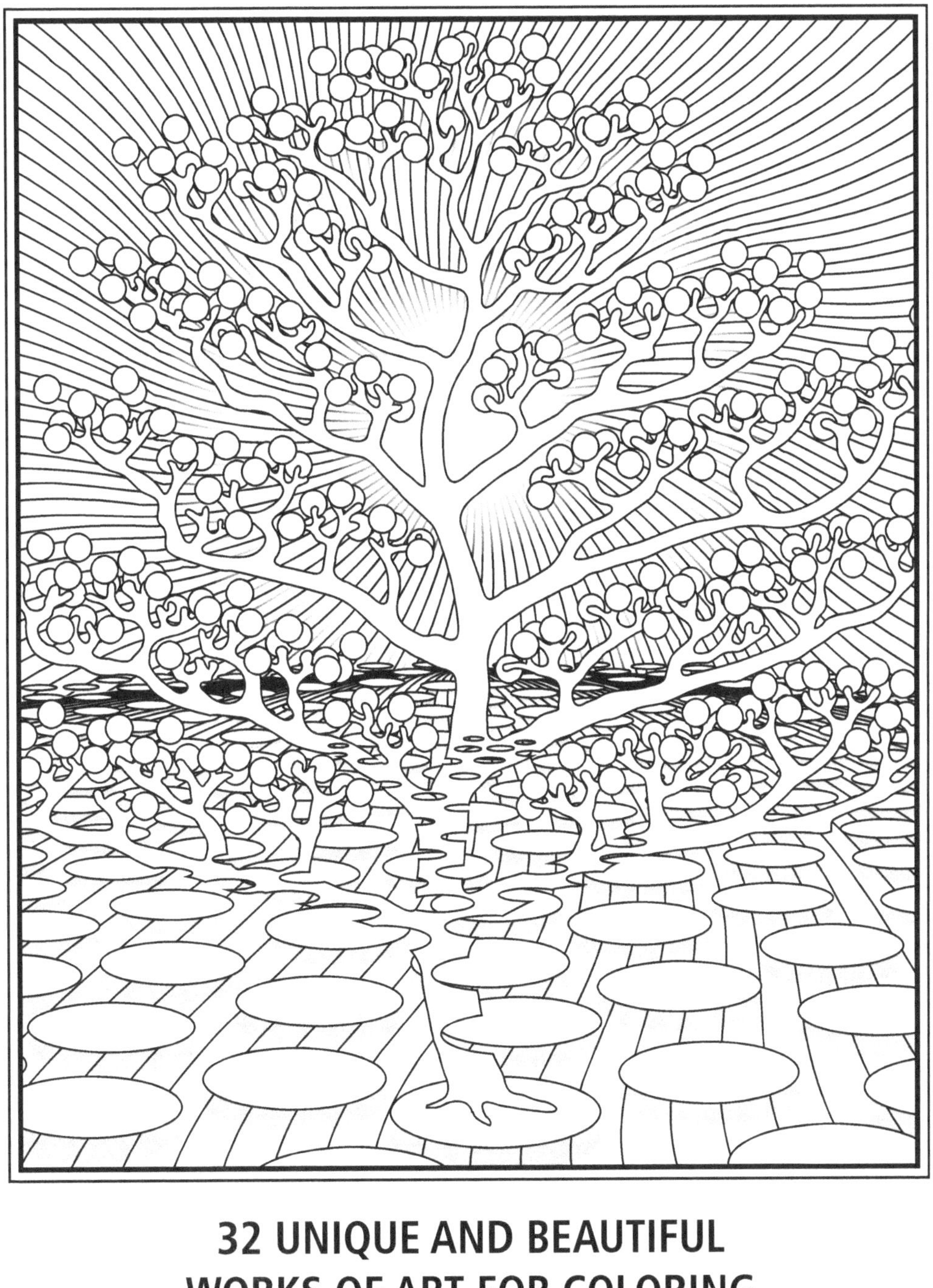

32 UNIQUE AND BEAUTIFUL WORKS OF ART FOR COLORING

by Gary Newman

Copyright © 2015 by Gary Newman

Phoenix Century Press
P.O. Box 1792
Sausalito, CA 94966

www.phoenixcenturypress.com

Layers of Reality:
32 Unique and Beautiful
Works of Art for Coloring
by Gary Newman

ISBN-10: 0-9897316-2-6
ISBN-13: 978-0-9897316-2-1

Illustrations, cover and interior design by Gary Newman
www.newmango.com

Printed in the United States of America

For Susan,
who helps me see the world
as a new adventure,
every day.

INTRODUCTION

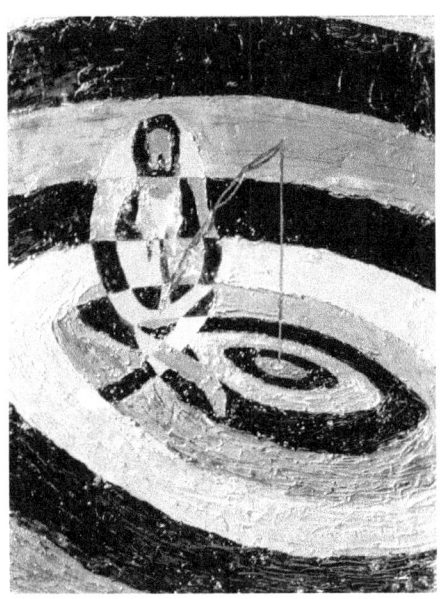

When I was in high school, I took a painting class at the local college. I had never done a real painting on canvas before, and didn't know the first thing about it. But when I began working out what I wanted to paint, it became my first exploration into layers of reality. Done in intense shades of blue and green, it depicted a fisherman who has fallen asleep on the bank of a lake. Where his fishing line enters the water, it creates dreamlike ripples that radiate outward to encompass the man and his world.

I've always been interested in how we perceive the world. If we walk along a forest trail thinking about the drama of our daily lives, it's easy to miss the amazing stories going on around us. We look at a pool of water and notice the leaves floating there, but we have to shift our focus to see the fish beneath the surface, and the way the sunlight strikes the rocks below. We shift again and observe the trees reflected in the pool's surface, and then the clouds in the sky behind the trees. Each of these layers can be examined separately, but together they make a complex picture of a part of reality that we might miss if we aren't paying attention.

We are reminded that there is often more to reality than what we see on the surface, and these hidden layers can lead to unexpected beauty.

The 32 line drawings in this book may be viewed in any of several ways. They can be regarded simply as works of art, black and white drawings, just as they are. Some of the more intricate illustrations can operate as puzzles, for you to find and illuminate the underlying structure. In this respect, you're encouraged to look past the superficial details and wonder: Is that a picture on the wall, or a window looking through the wall? Which is the foreground, and which the background? Where does one layer end and the next begin?

And finally, they can be enjoyed simply as stress-relieving drawings to color. The drawn shapes are intended as guides; it isn't necessary to color each one individually (unless you want to). Remember that sometimes white is the best color. Relax. Let it flow. There is no right or wrong way.

At some point you may wish you could start over on a drawing, or try a different approach. Just for you, this volume includes a bonus second-chance section. All 32 drawings are reproduced again in the second half of the book, so you may try a new color scheme, if you desire.

Some of the drawings are simple and fanciful while others are more challenging. They are all unfinished works of art. I invite you to bring the artwork to completion by adding the color that will help define the layers of reality.

I would very much like to see the results of your coloring. Please feel free to photograph your work and share it on the book's Facebook page.

Good luck and happy coloring!

Gary Newman

ILLUSTRATION LIST

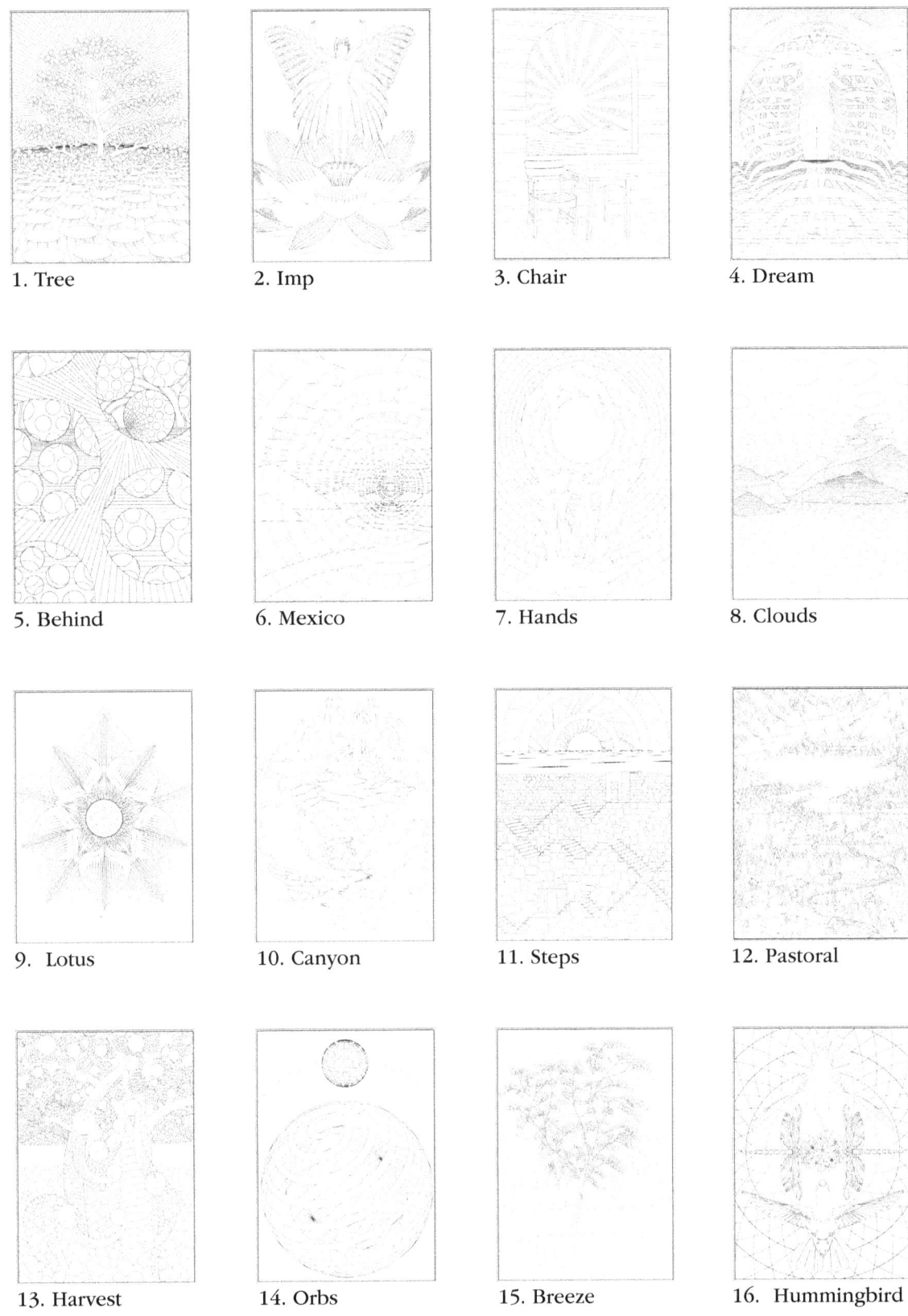

1. Tree

2. Imp

3. Chair

4. Dream

5. Behind

6. Mexico

7. Hands

8. Clouds

9. Lotus

10. Canyon

11. Steps

12. Pastoral

13. Harvest

14. Orbs

15. Breeze

16. Hummingbird

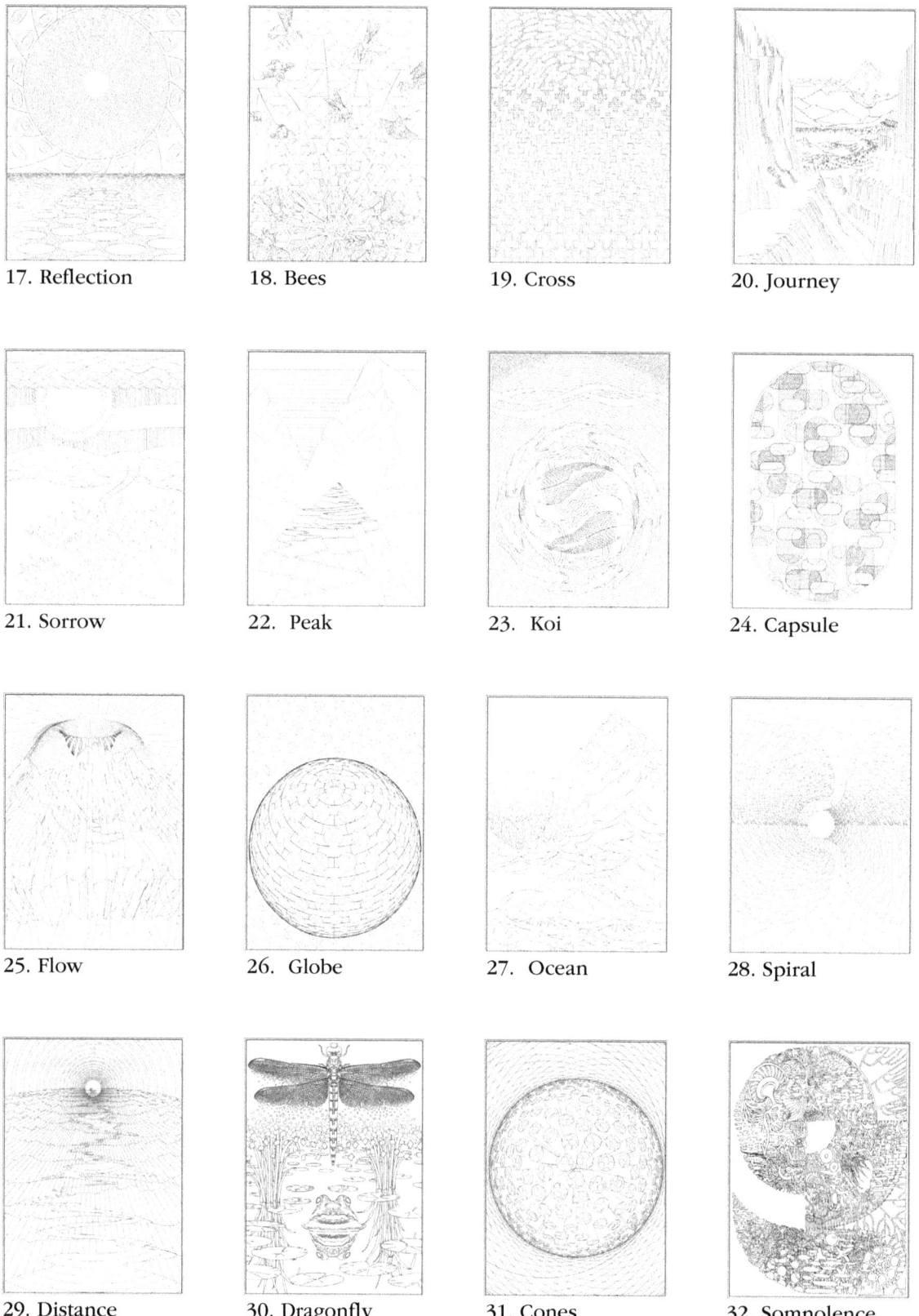

17. Reflection

18. Bees

19. Cross

20. Journey

21. Sorrow

22. Peak

23. Koi

24. Capsule

25. Flow

26. Globe

27. Ocean

28. Spiral

29. Distance

30. Dragonfly

31. Cones

32. Somnolence

Section I
The Drawings

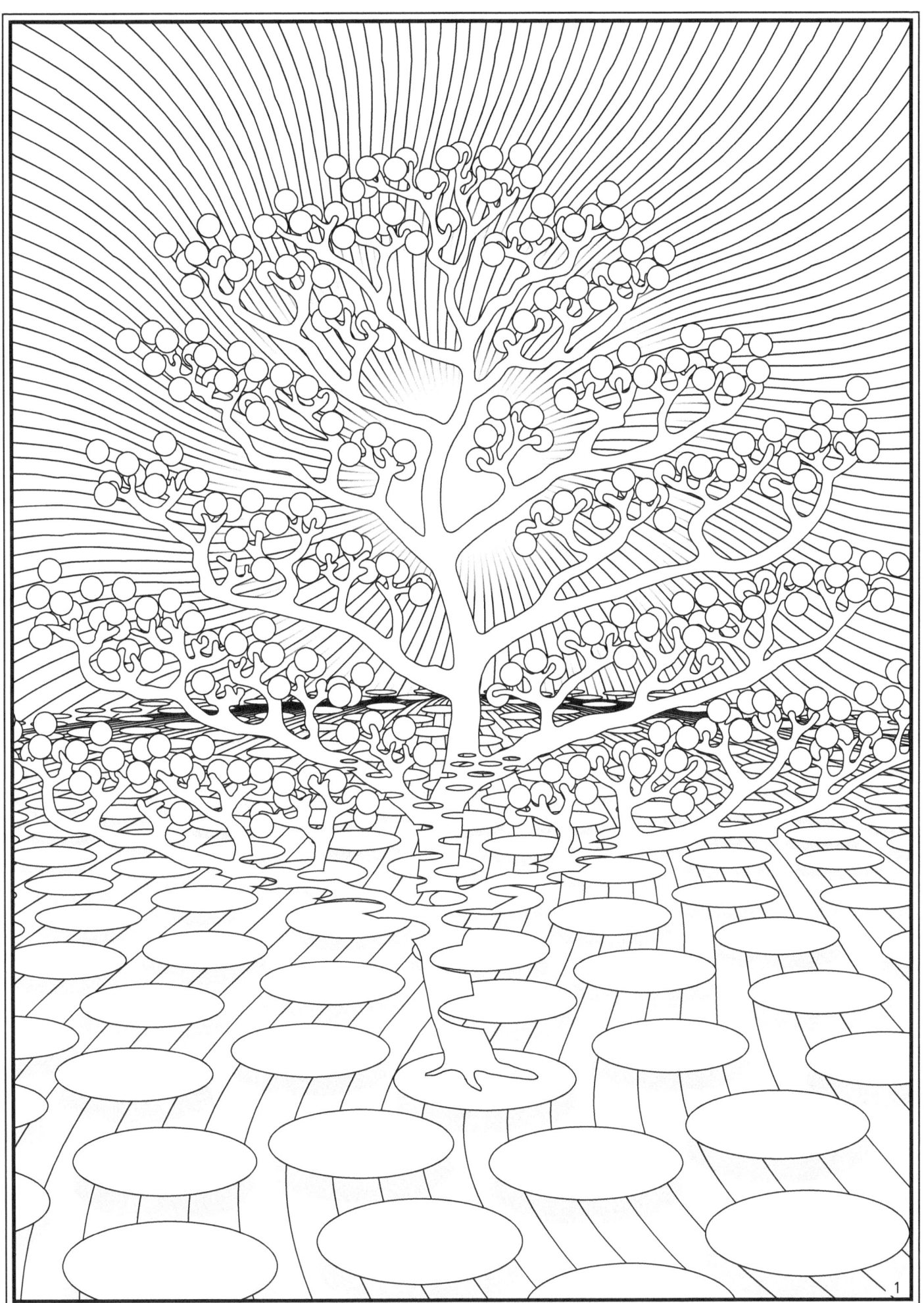

1

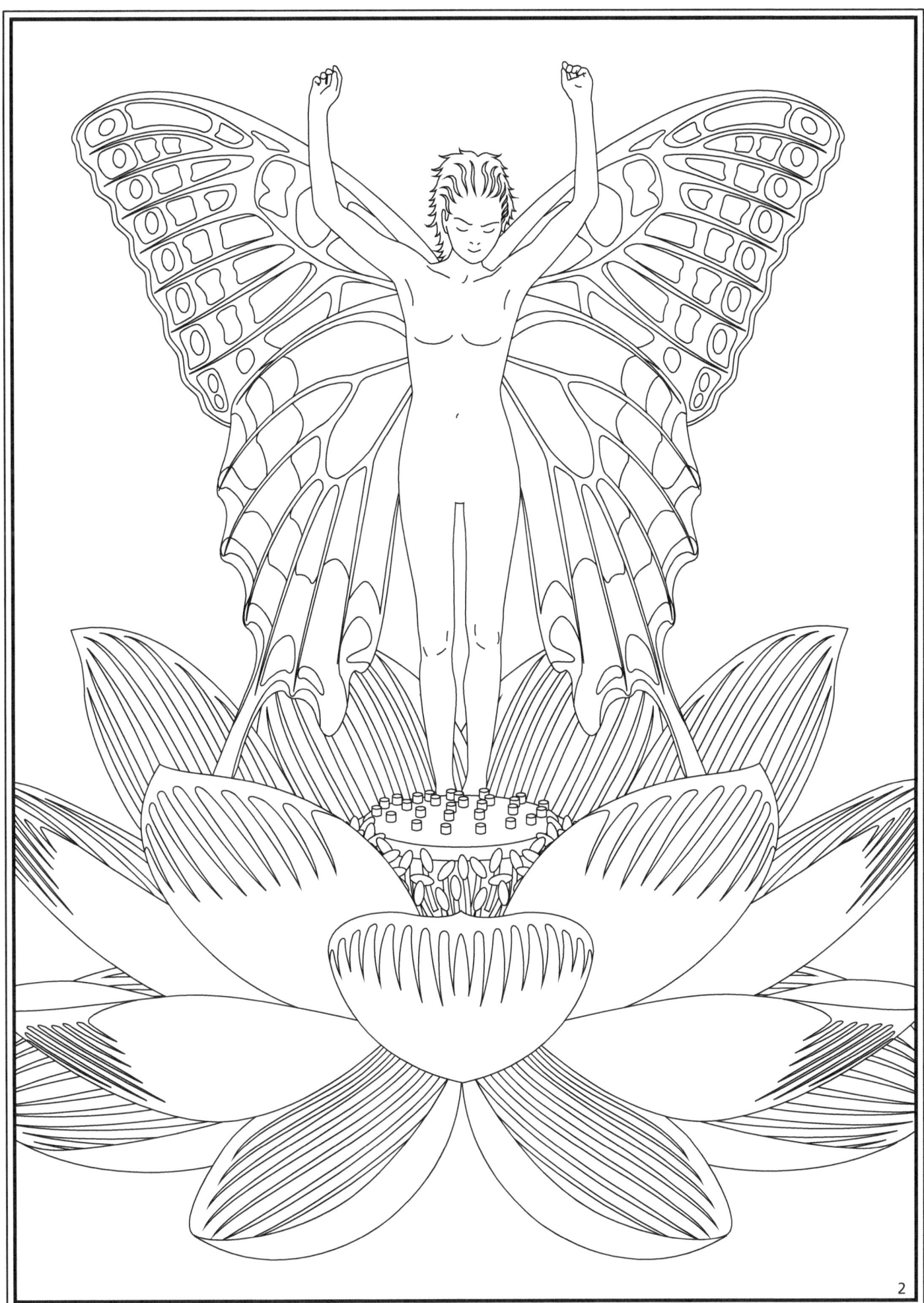

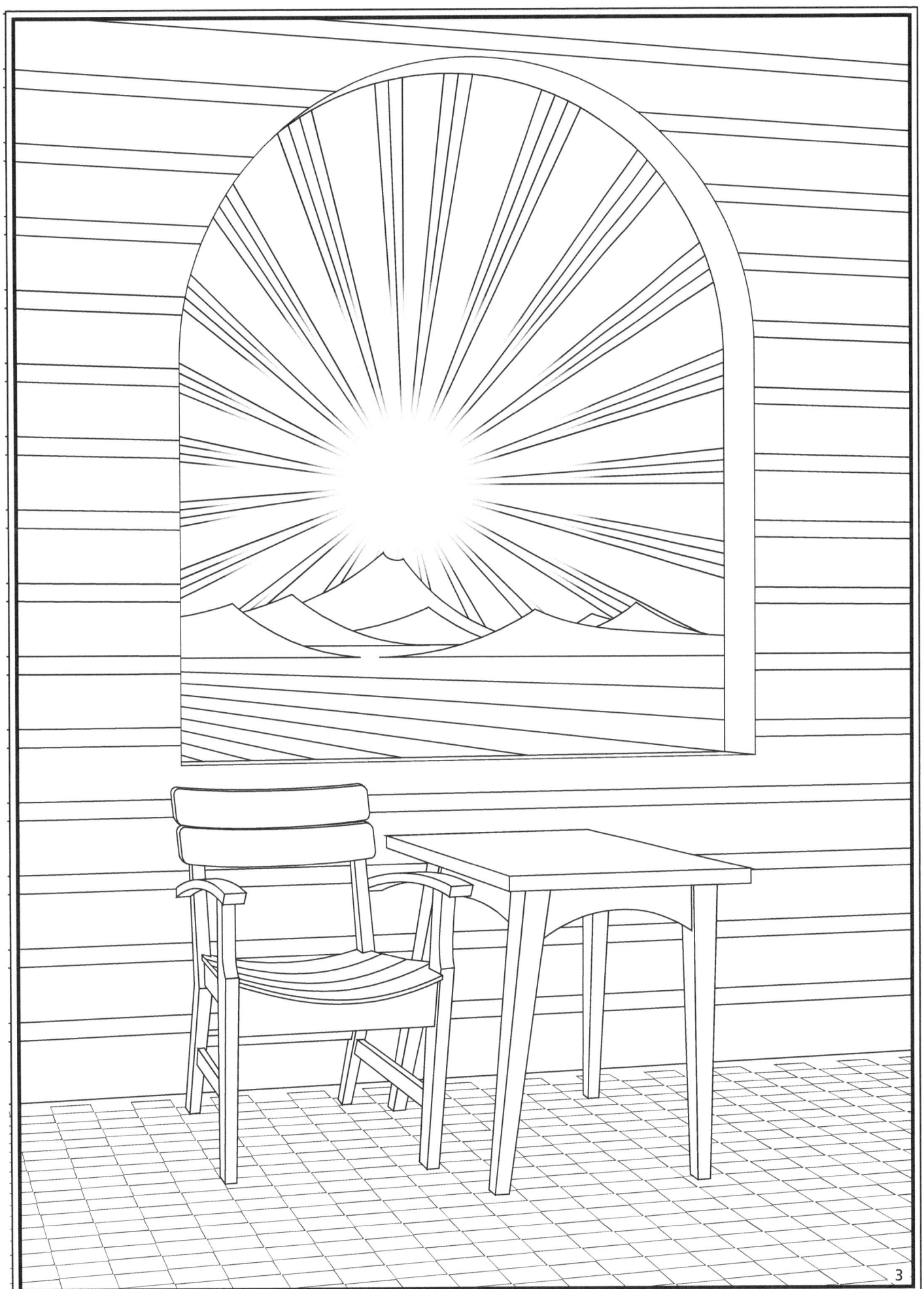

3

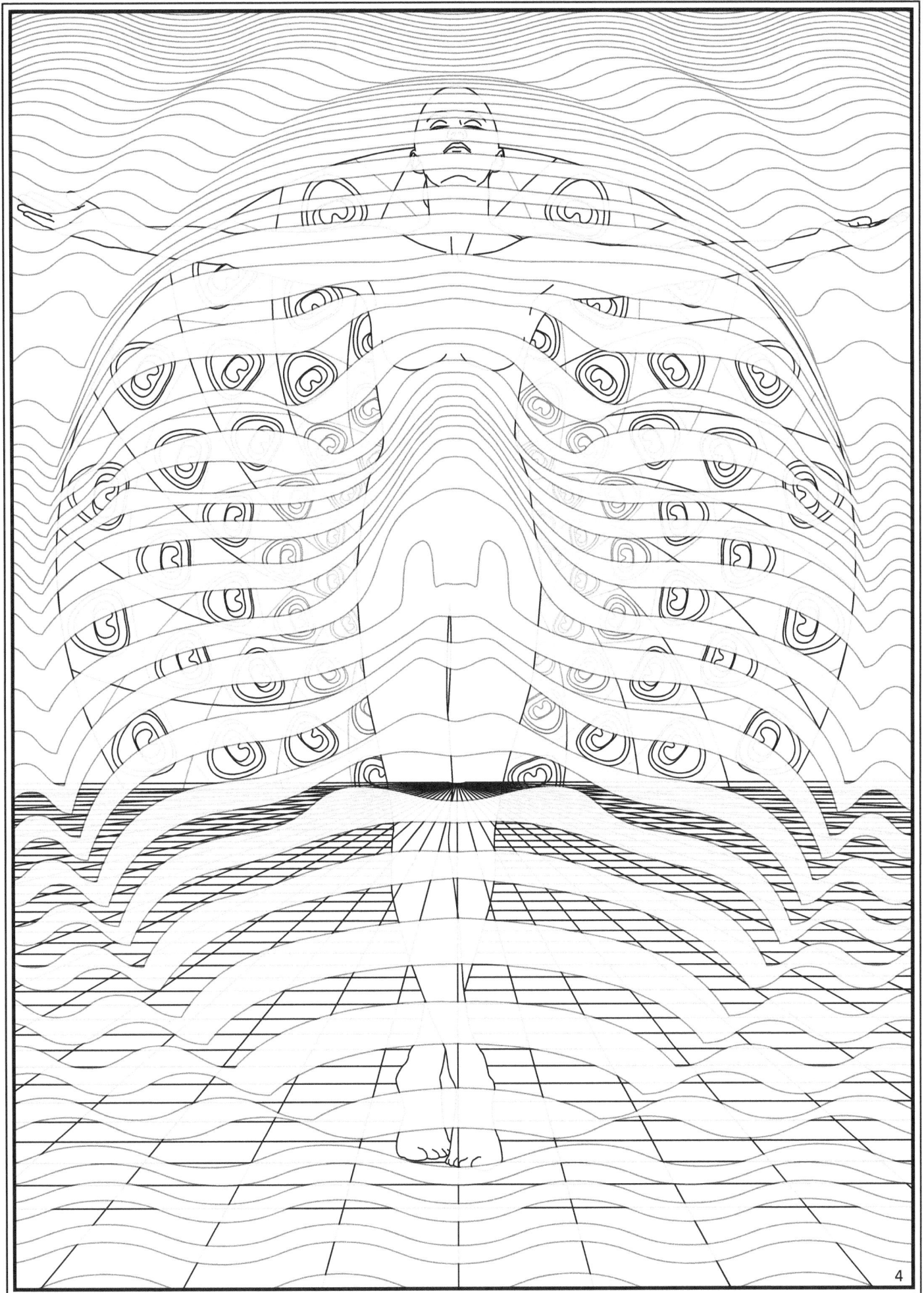

4

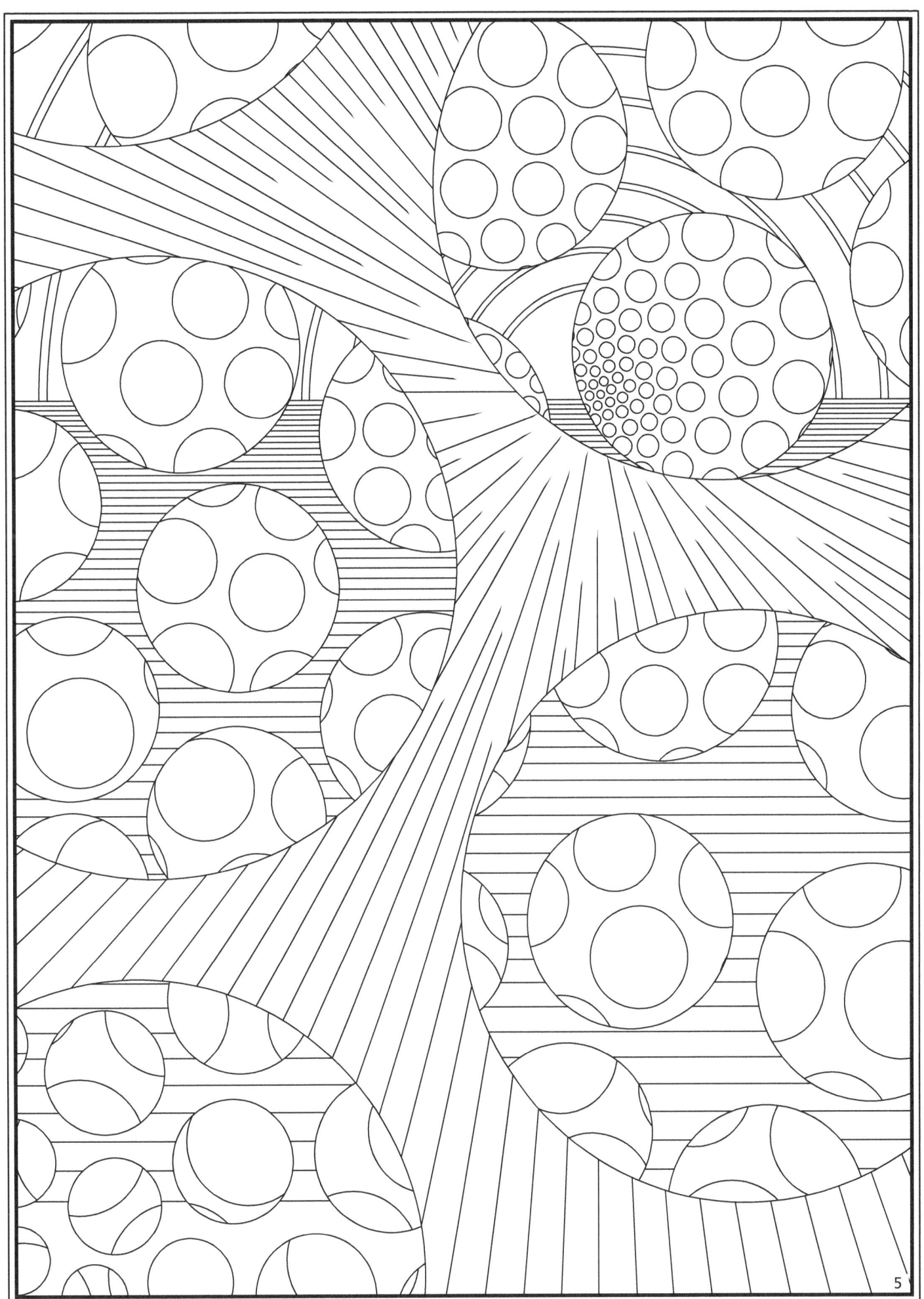

5

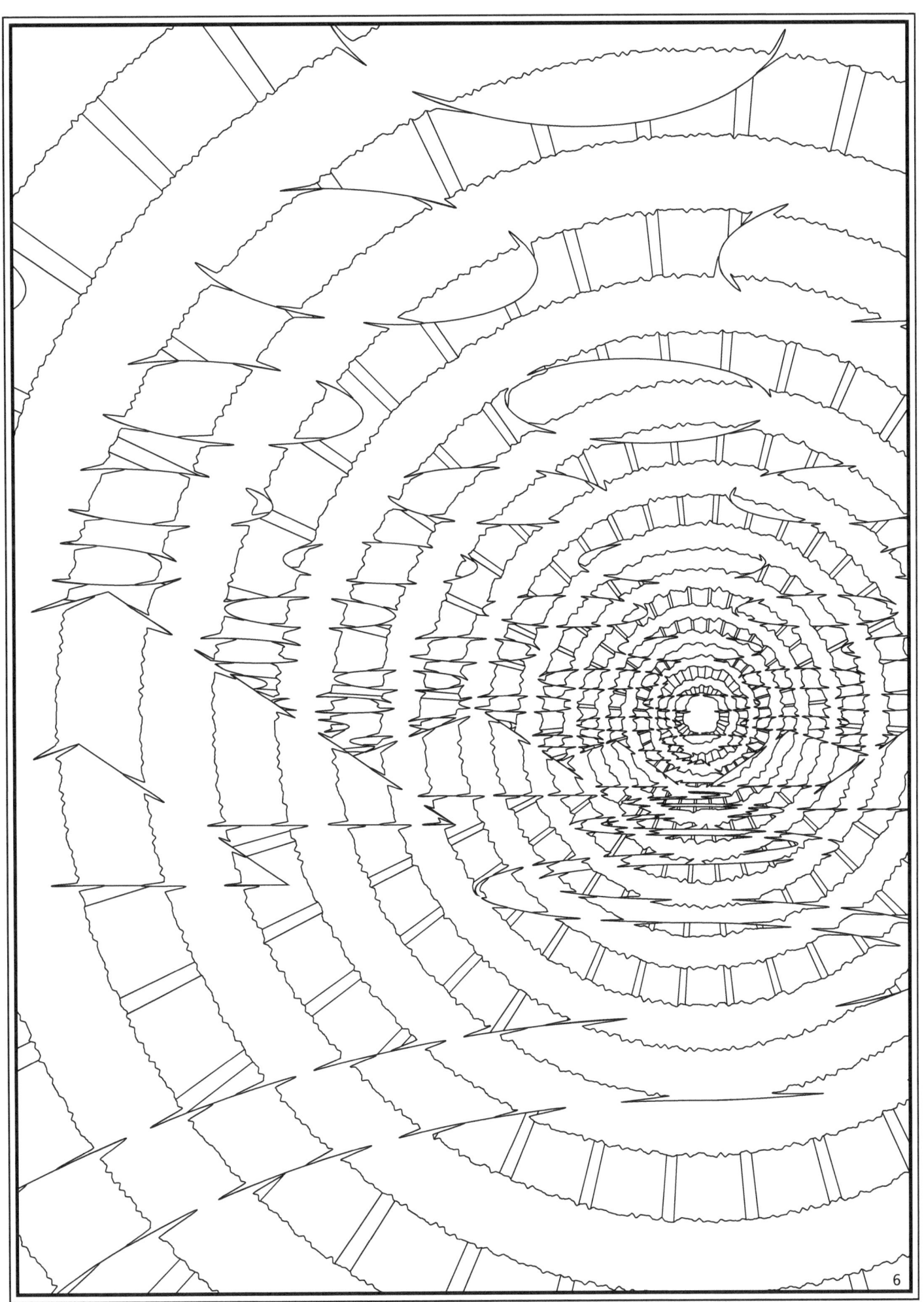

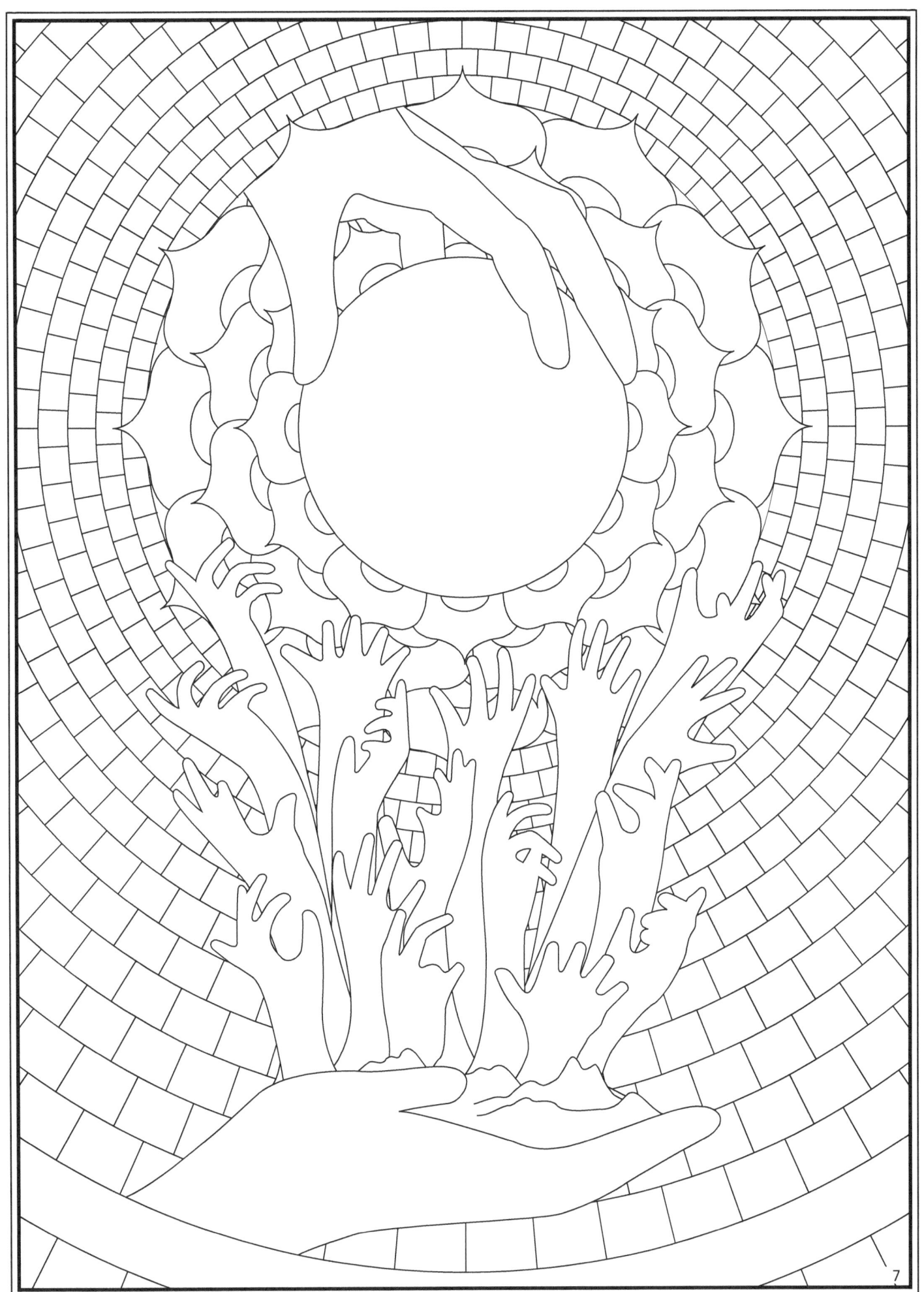

7

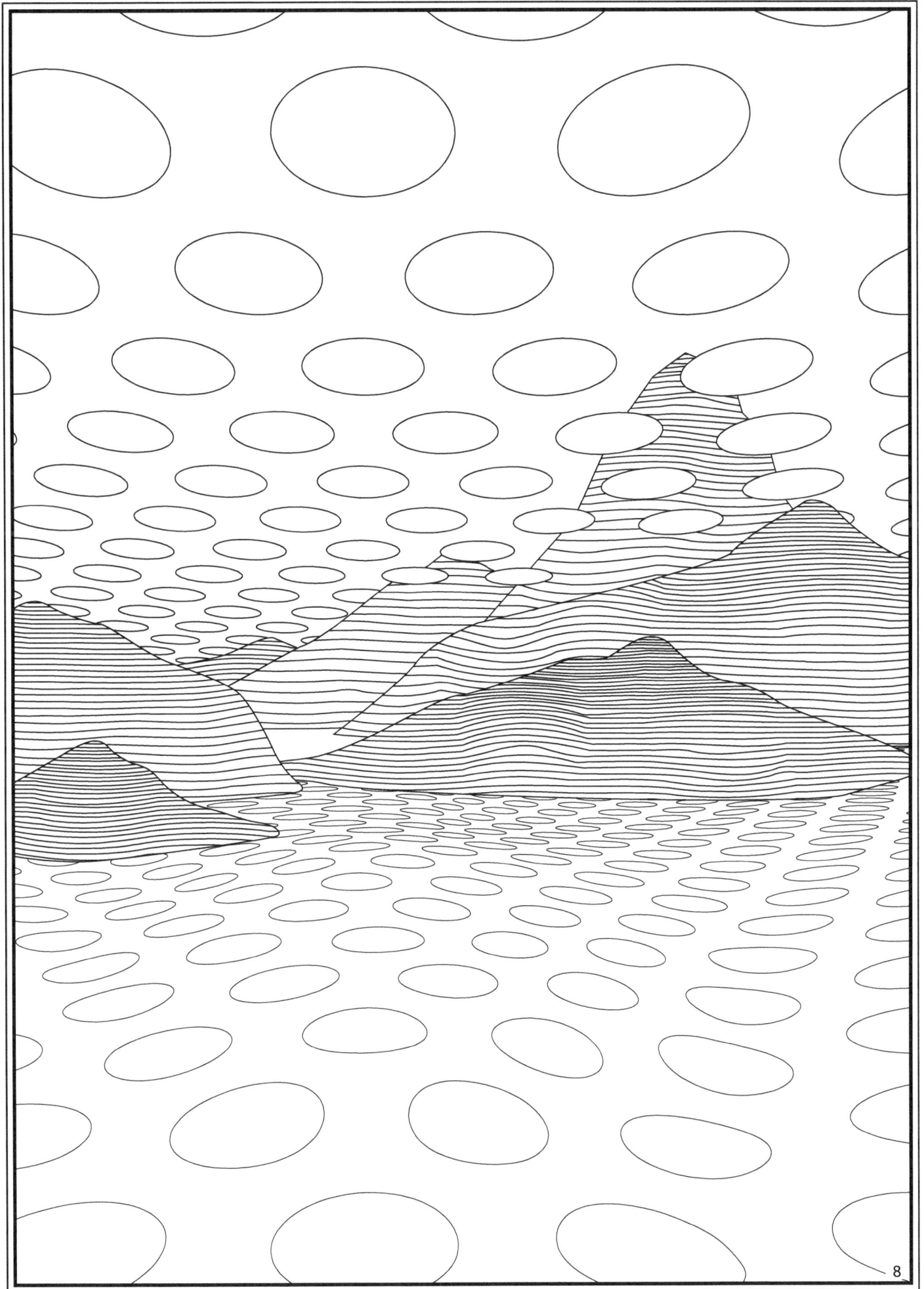

8

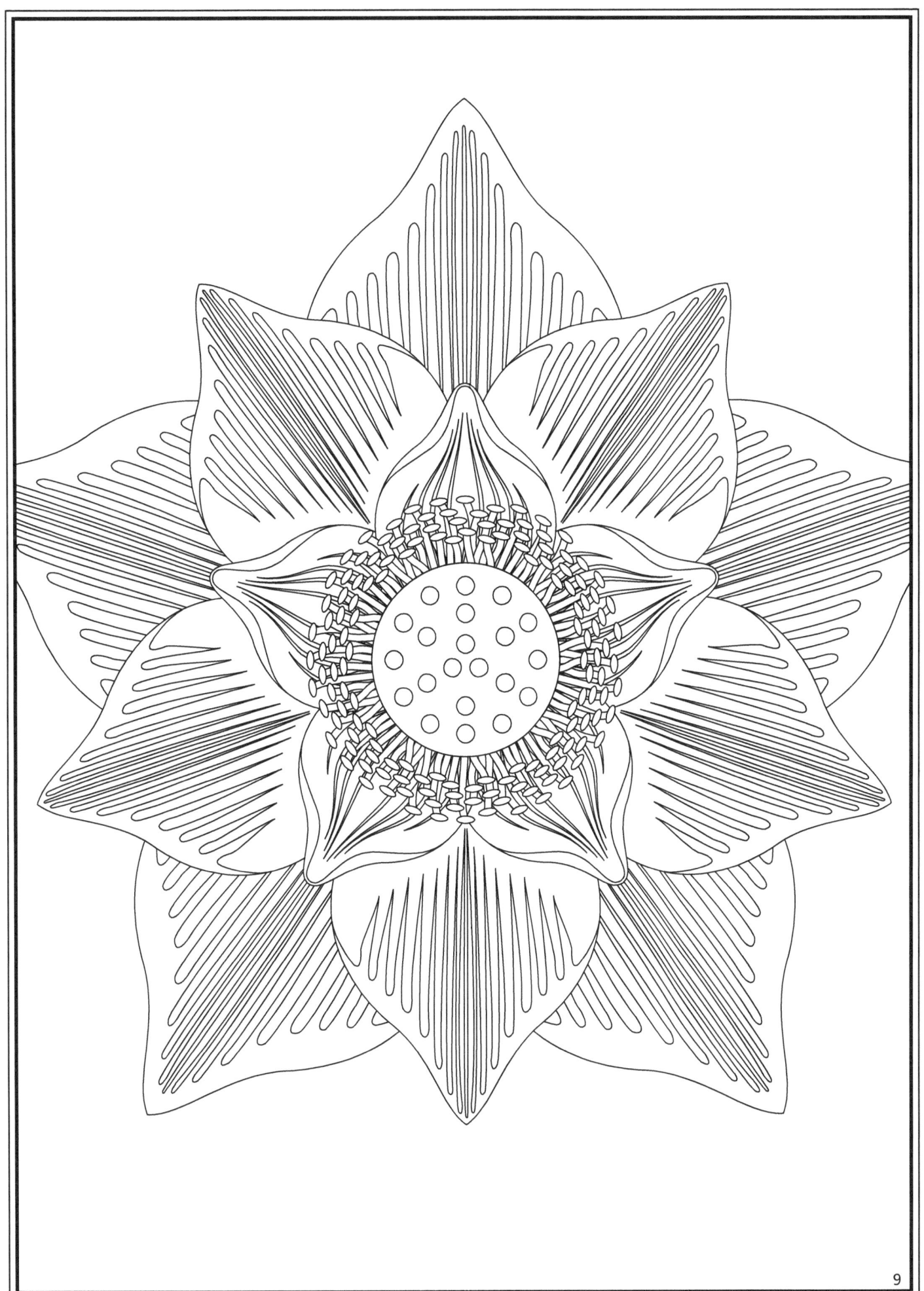

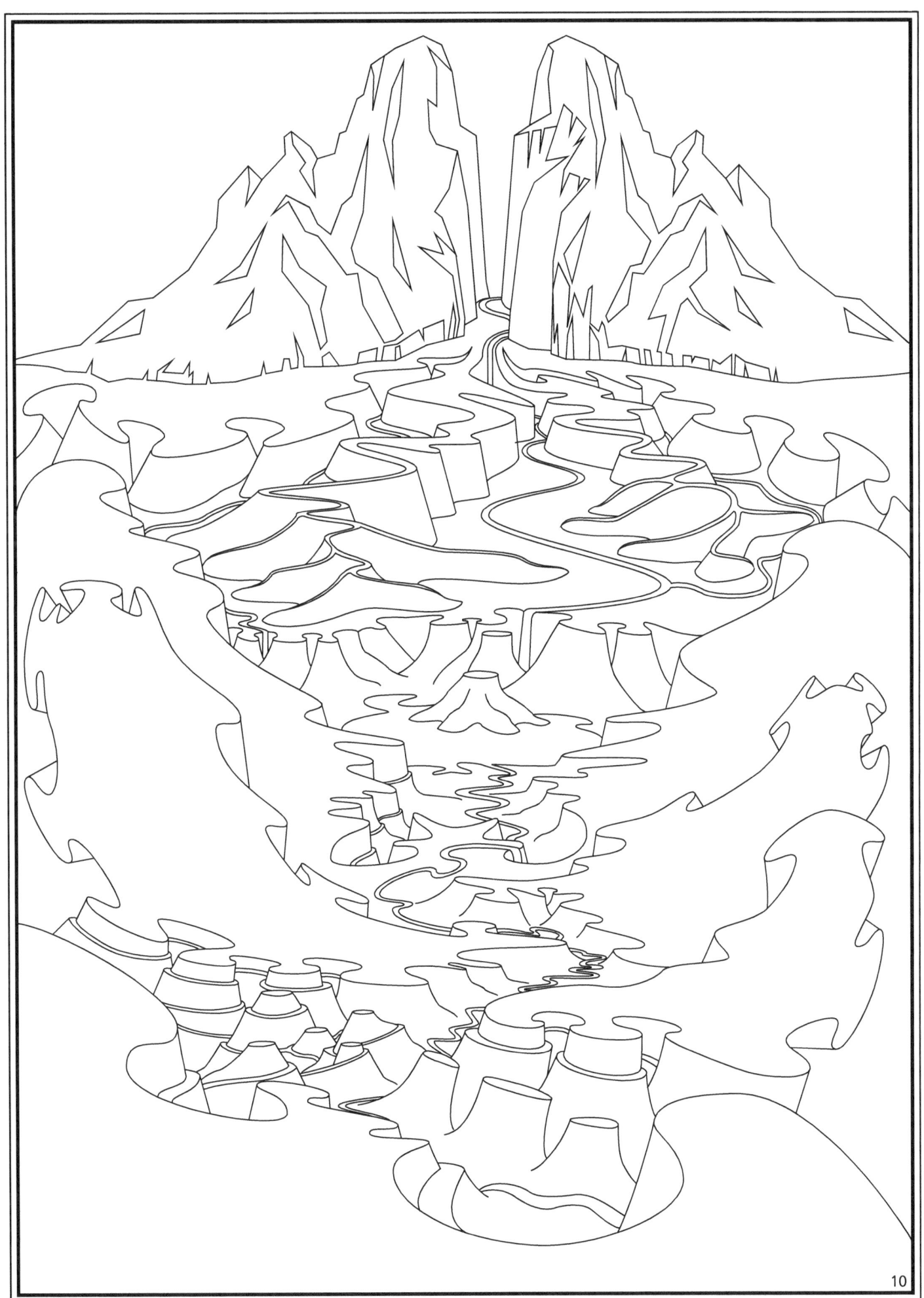

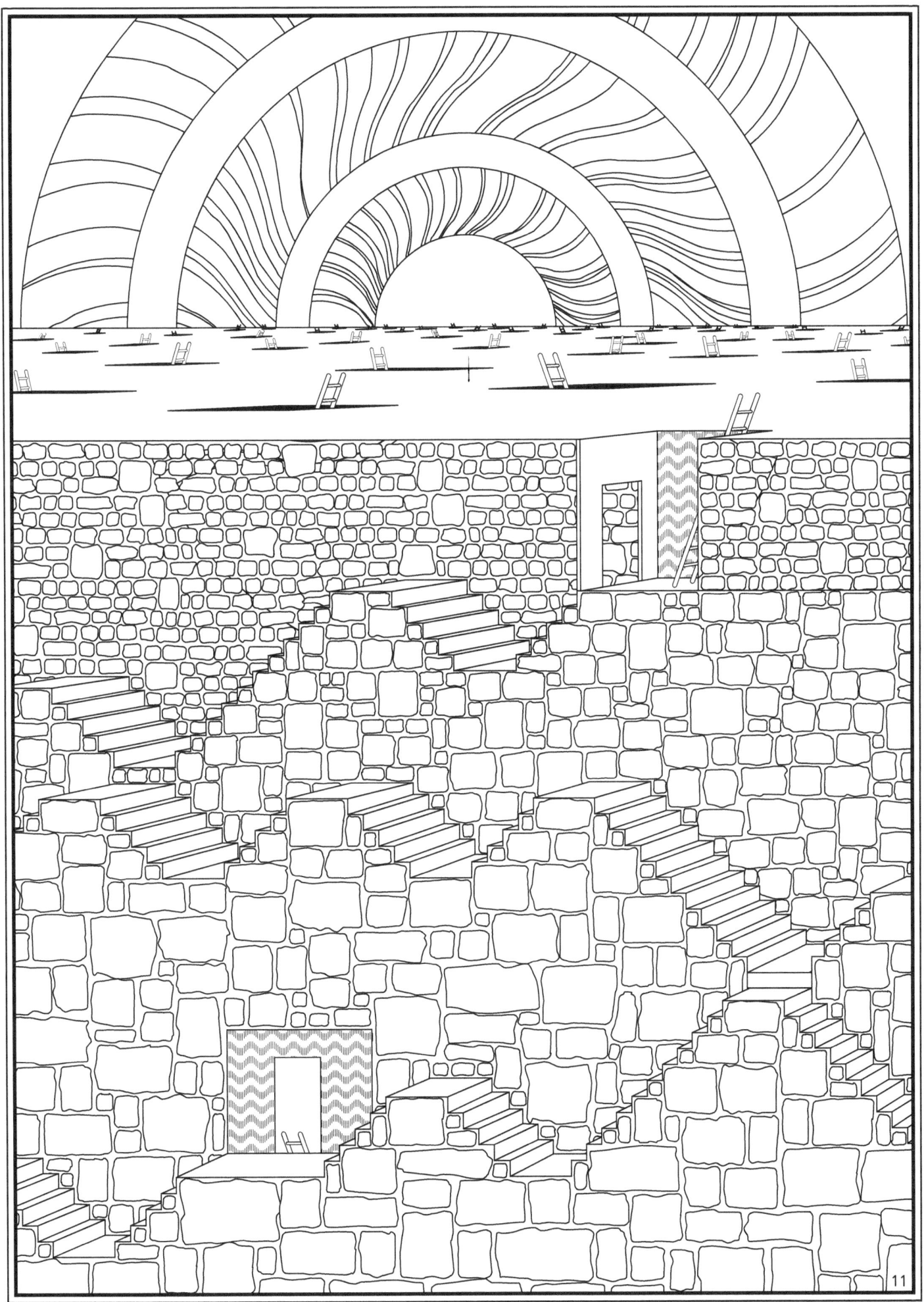

11

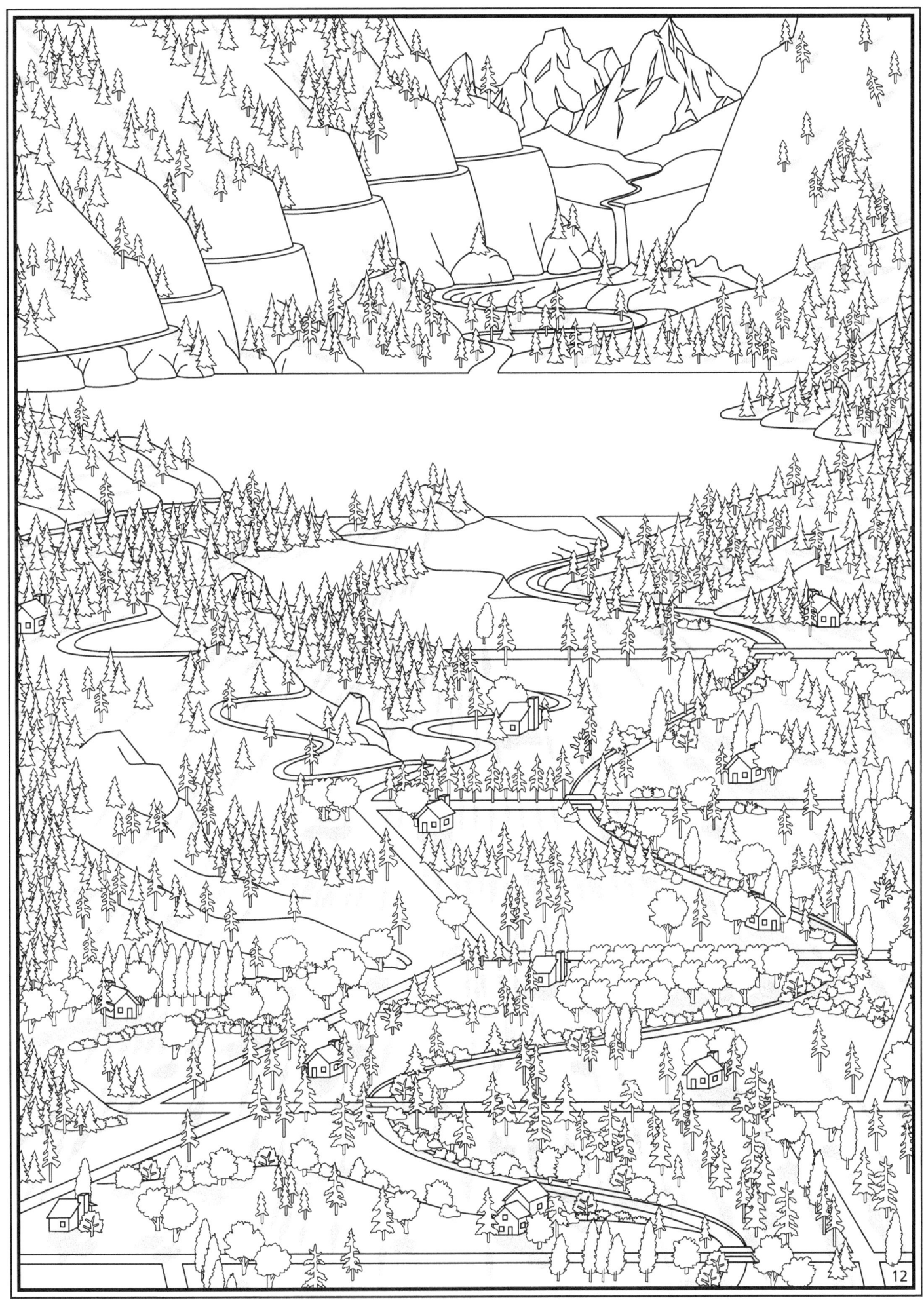

12

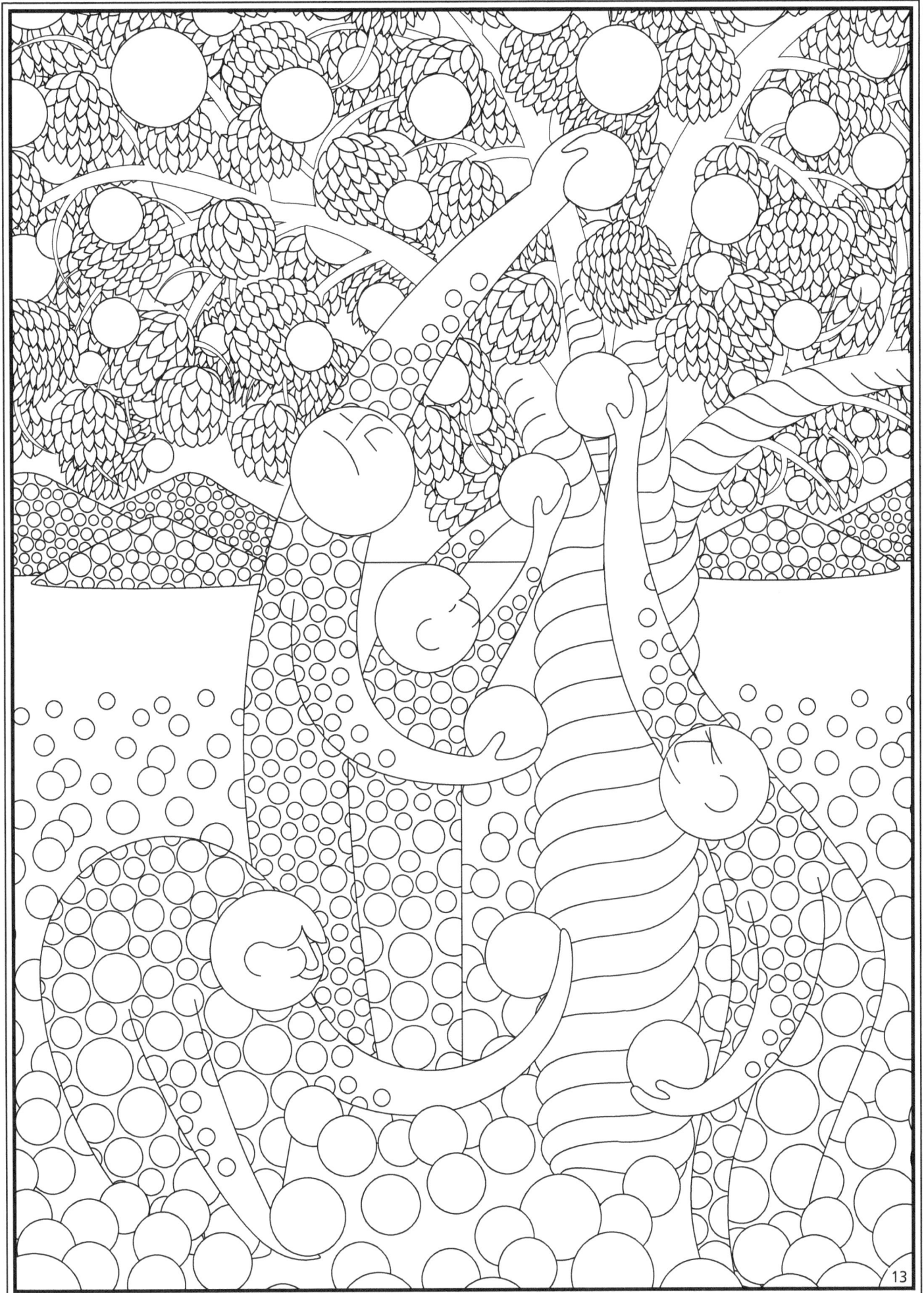

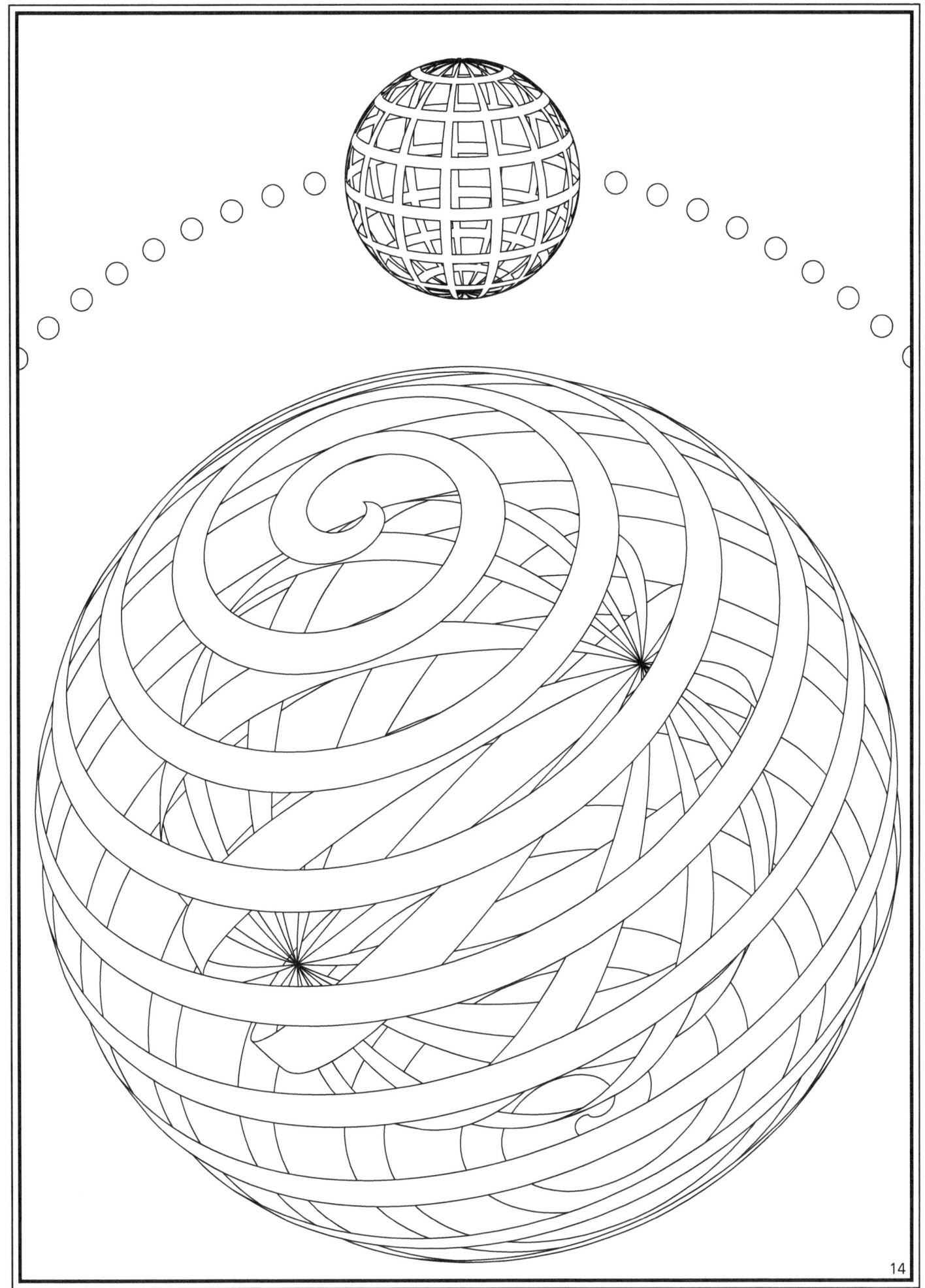

14

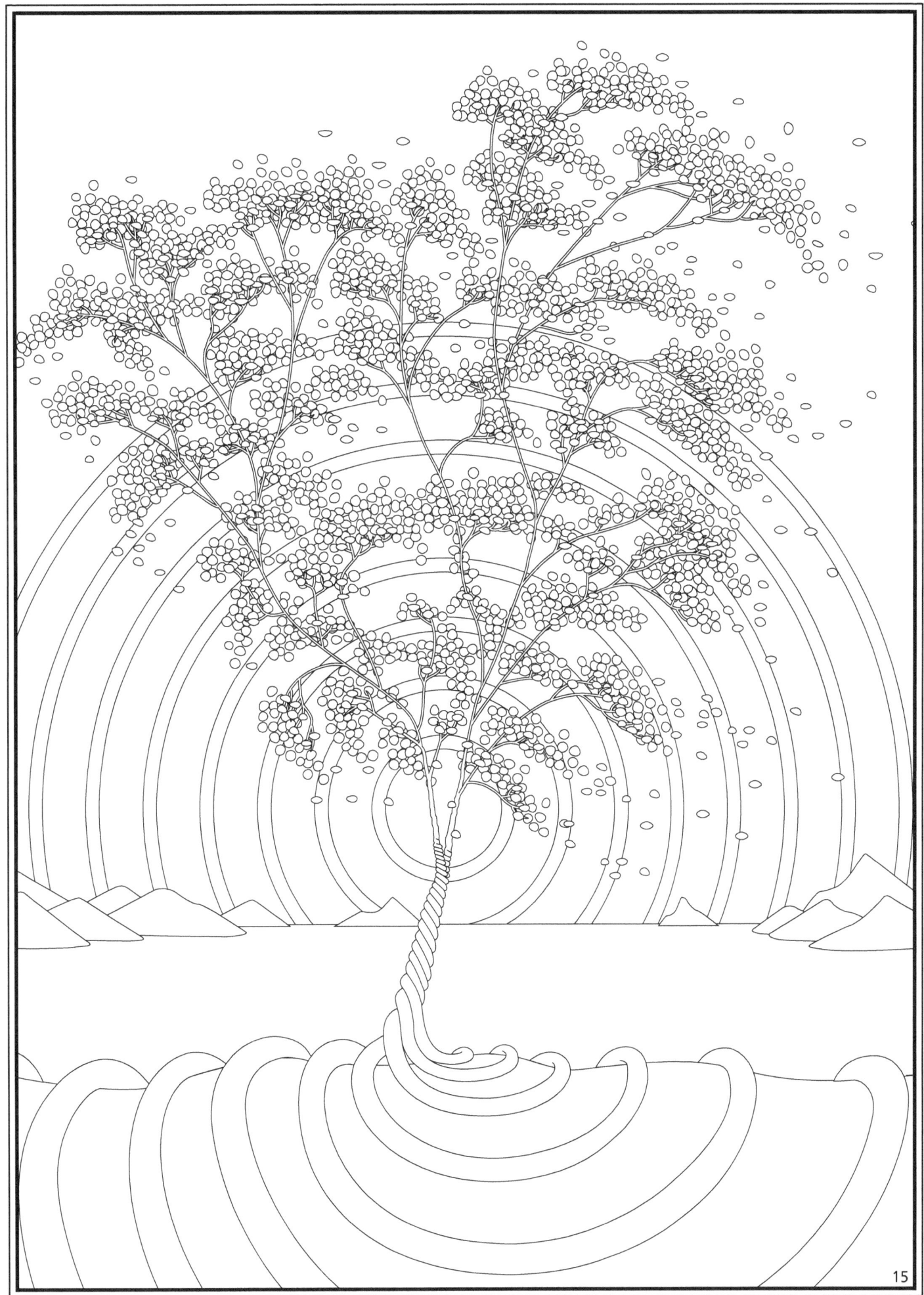

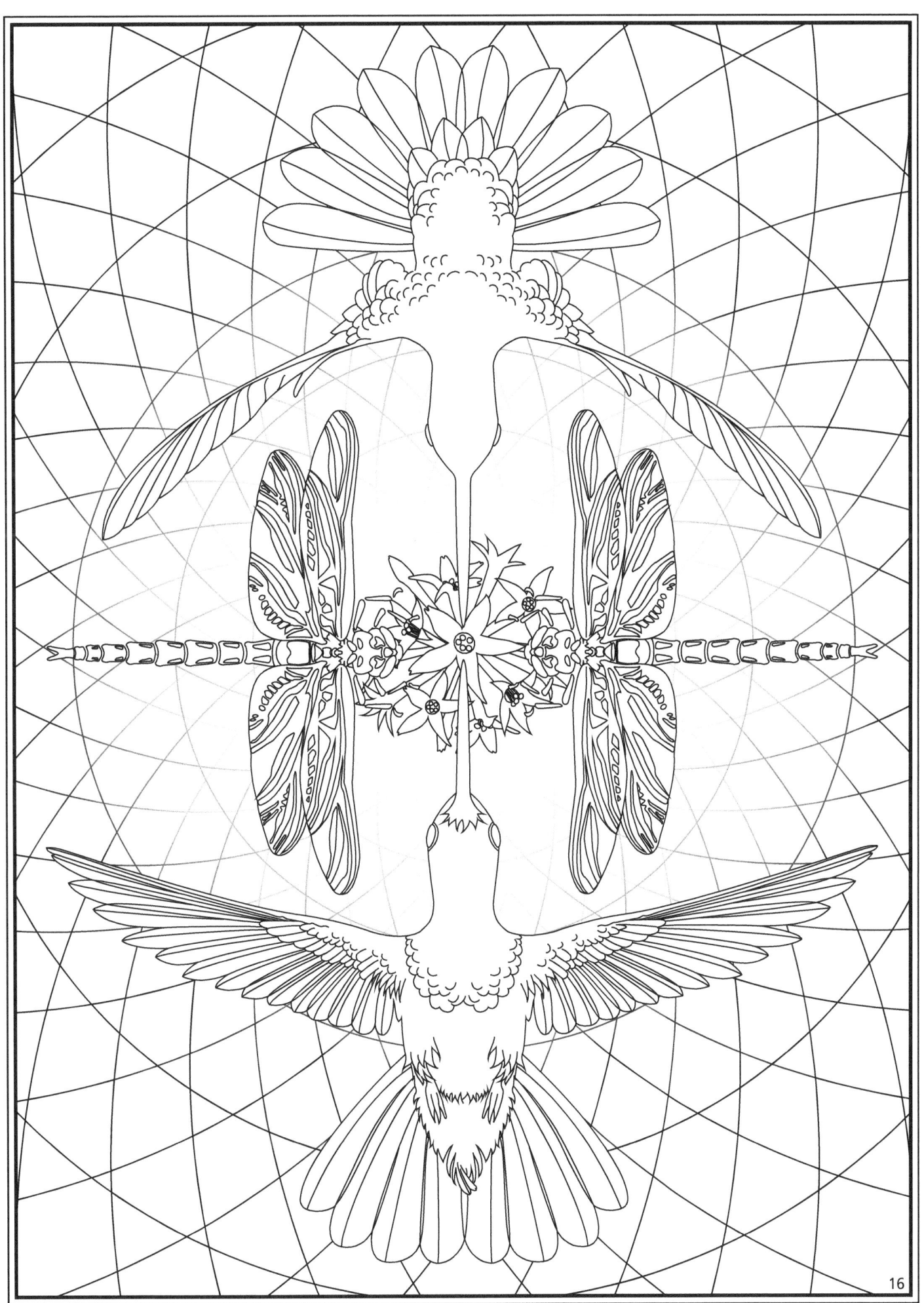

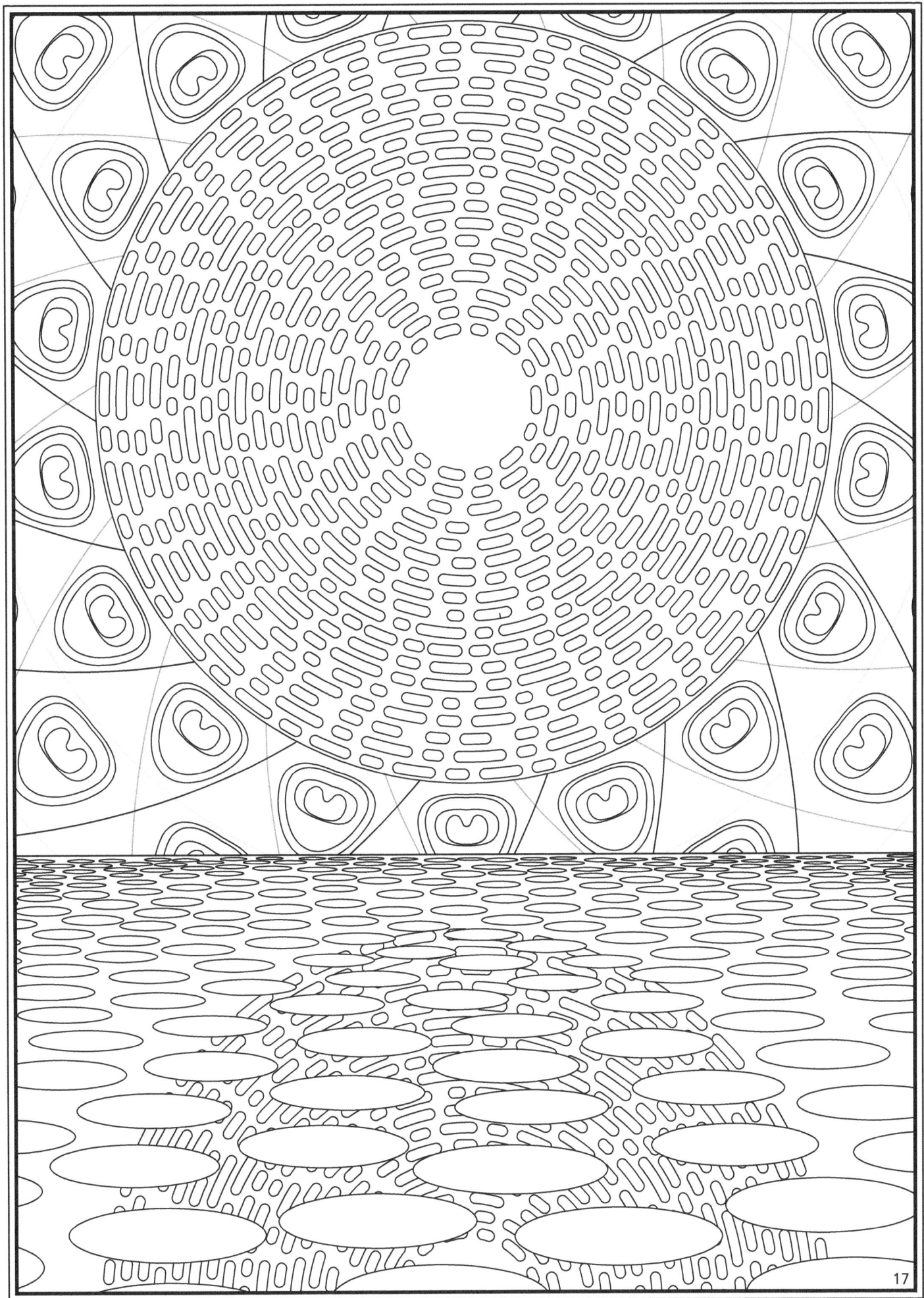

17

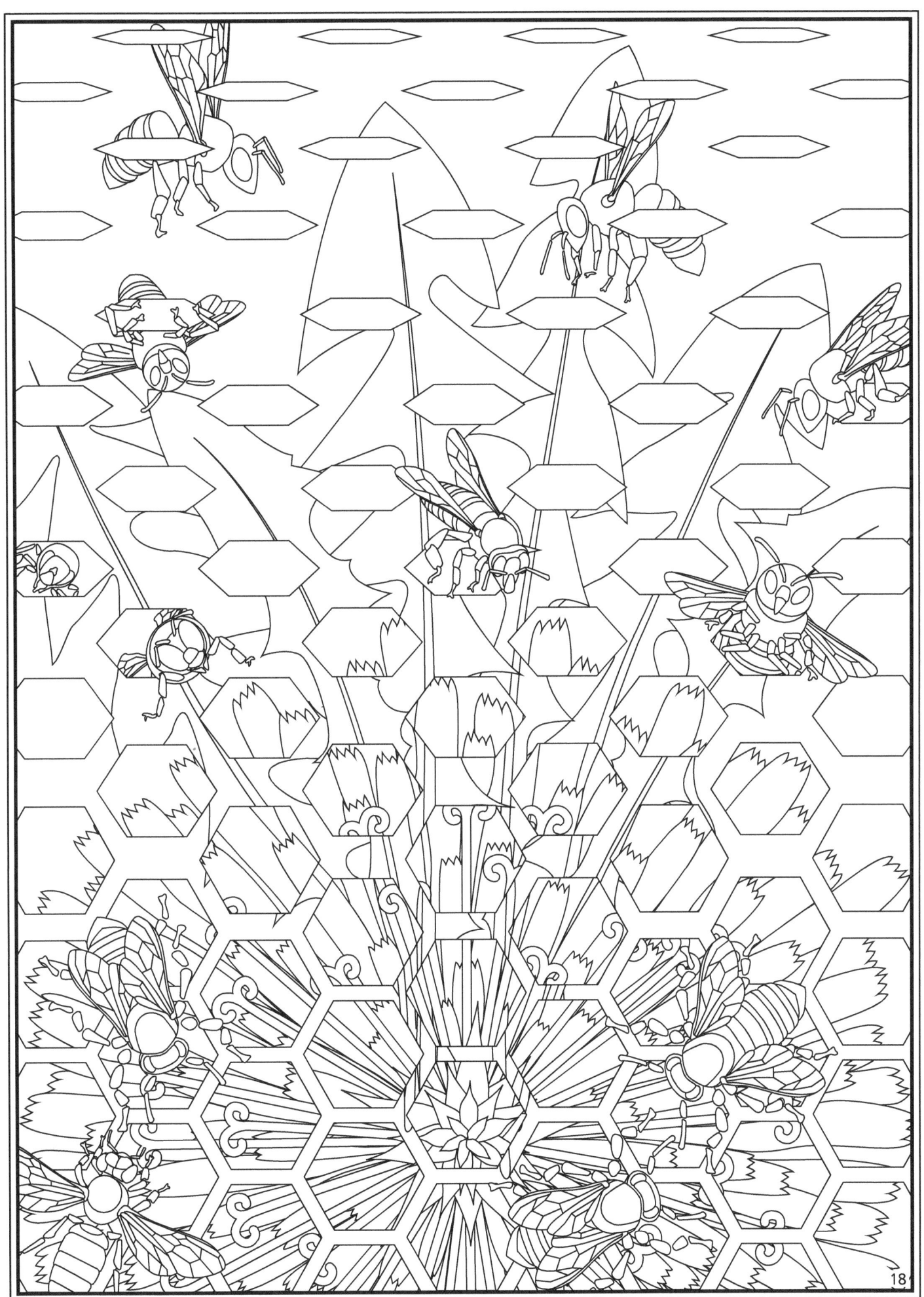

18

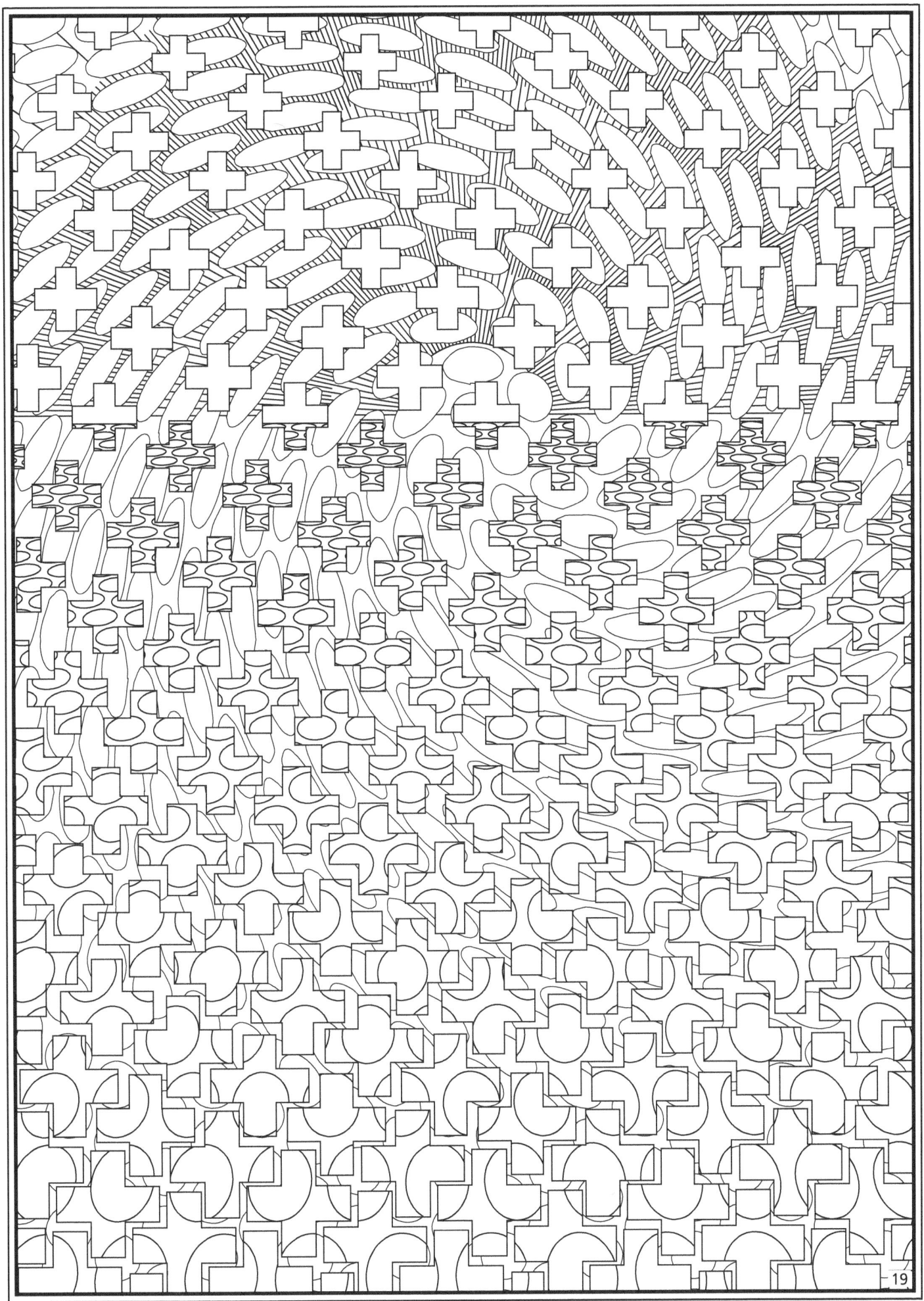

19

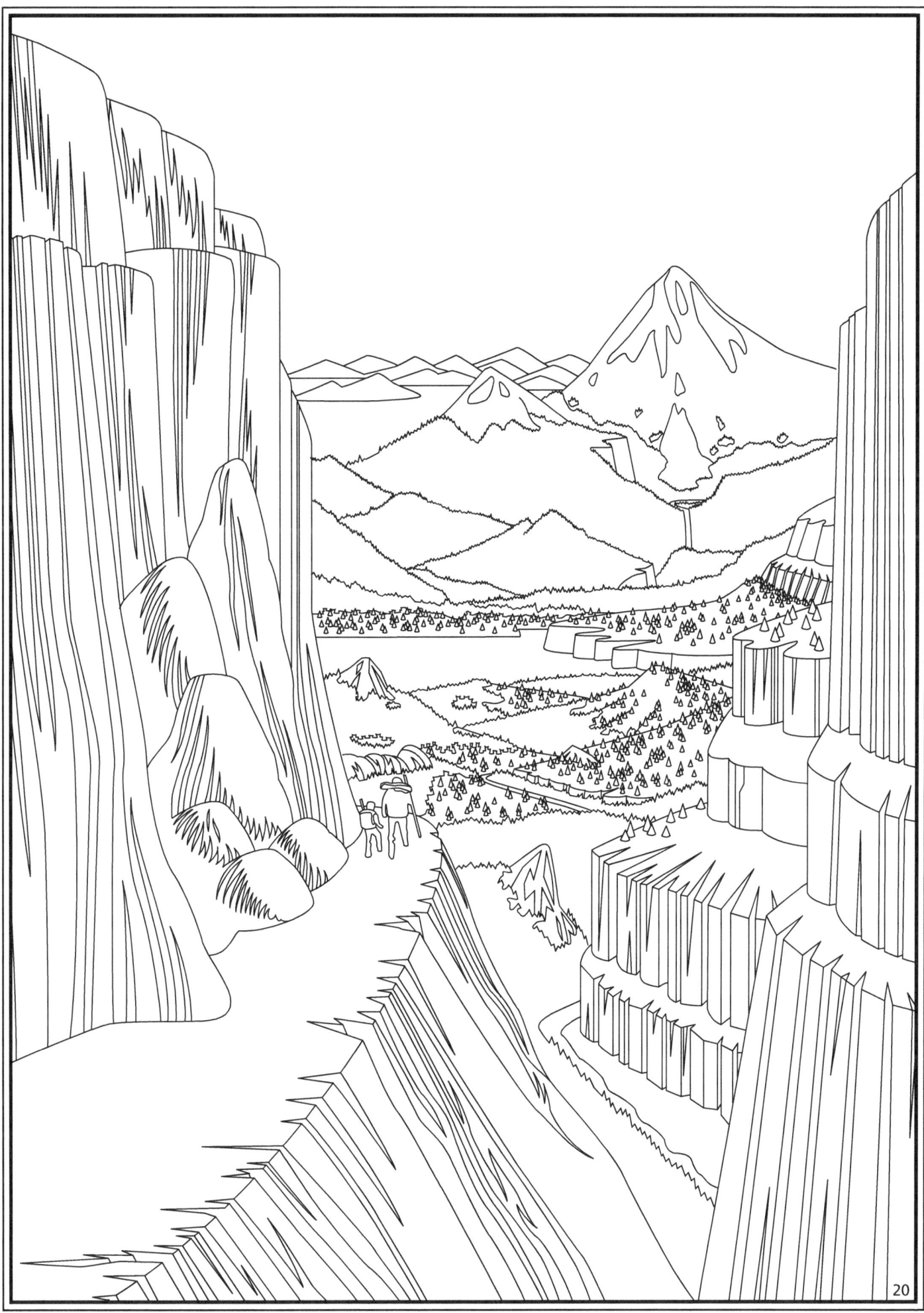

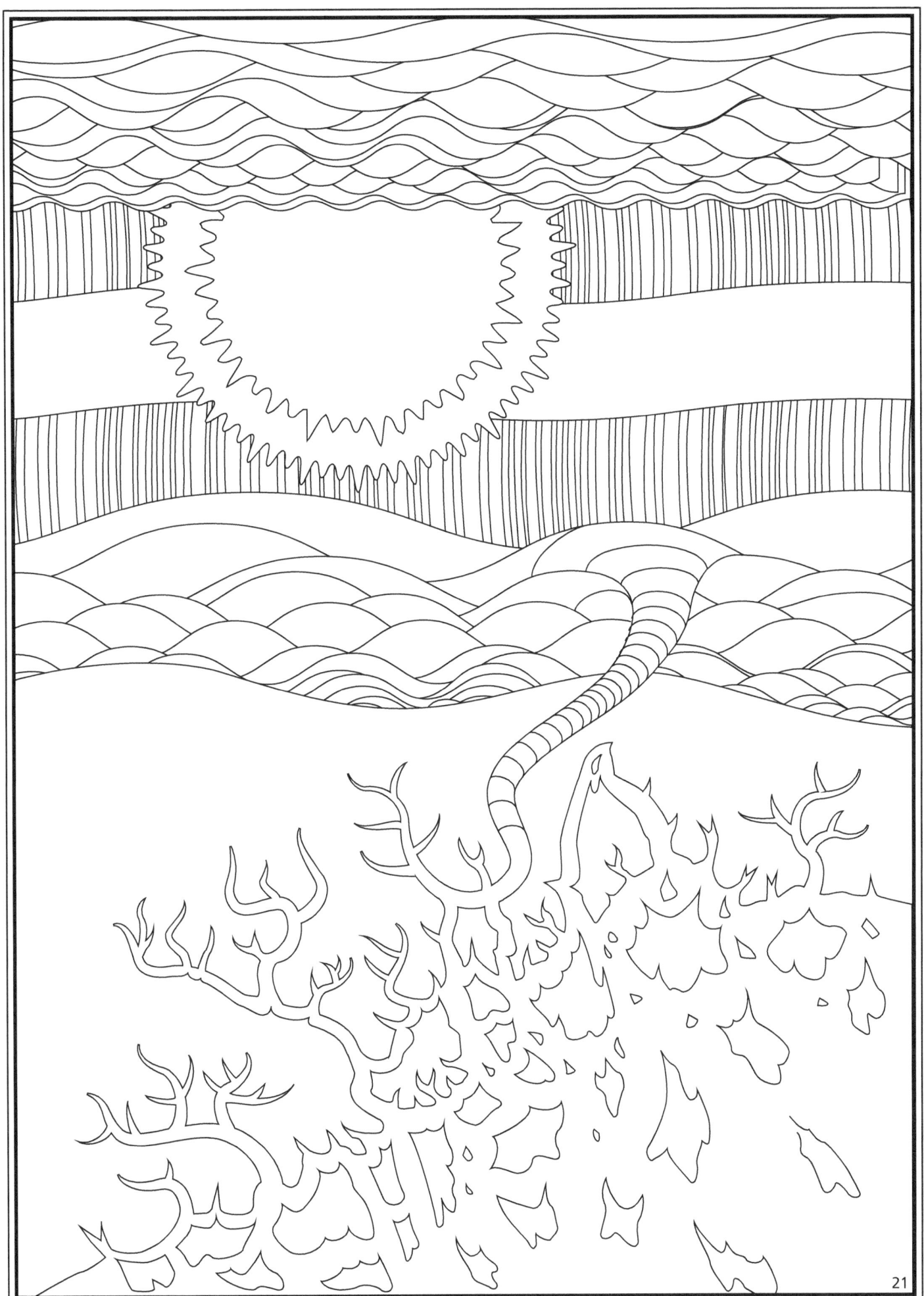

21

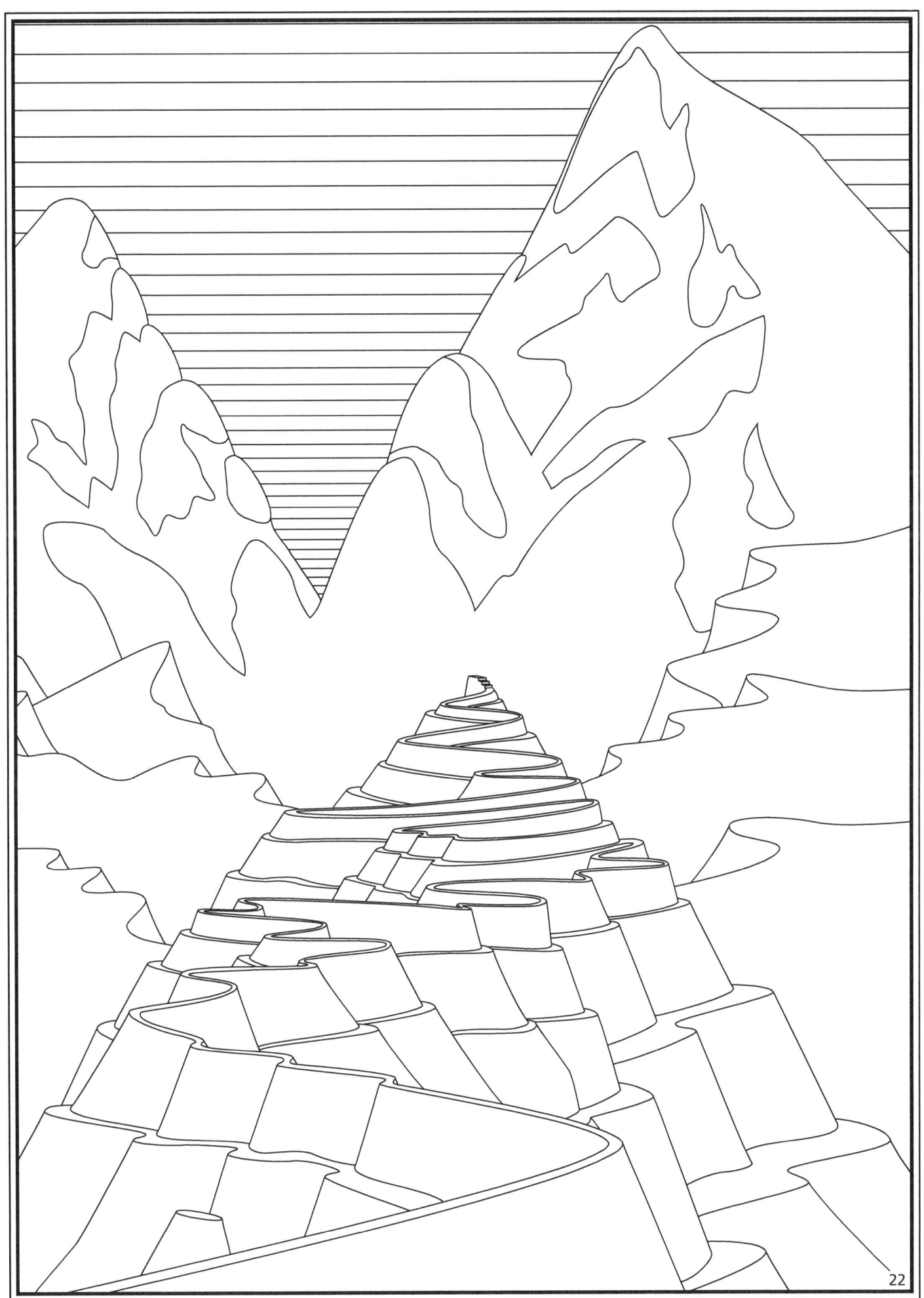

22

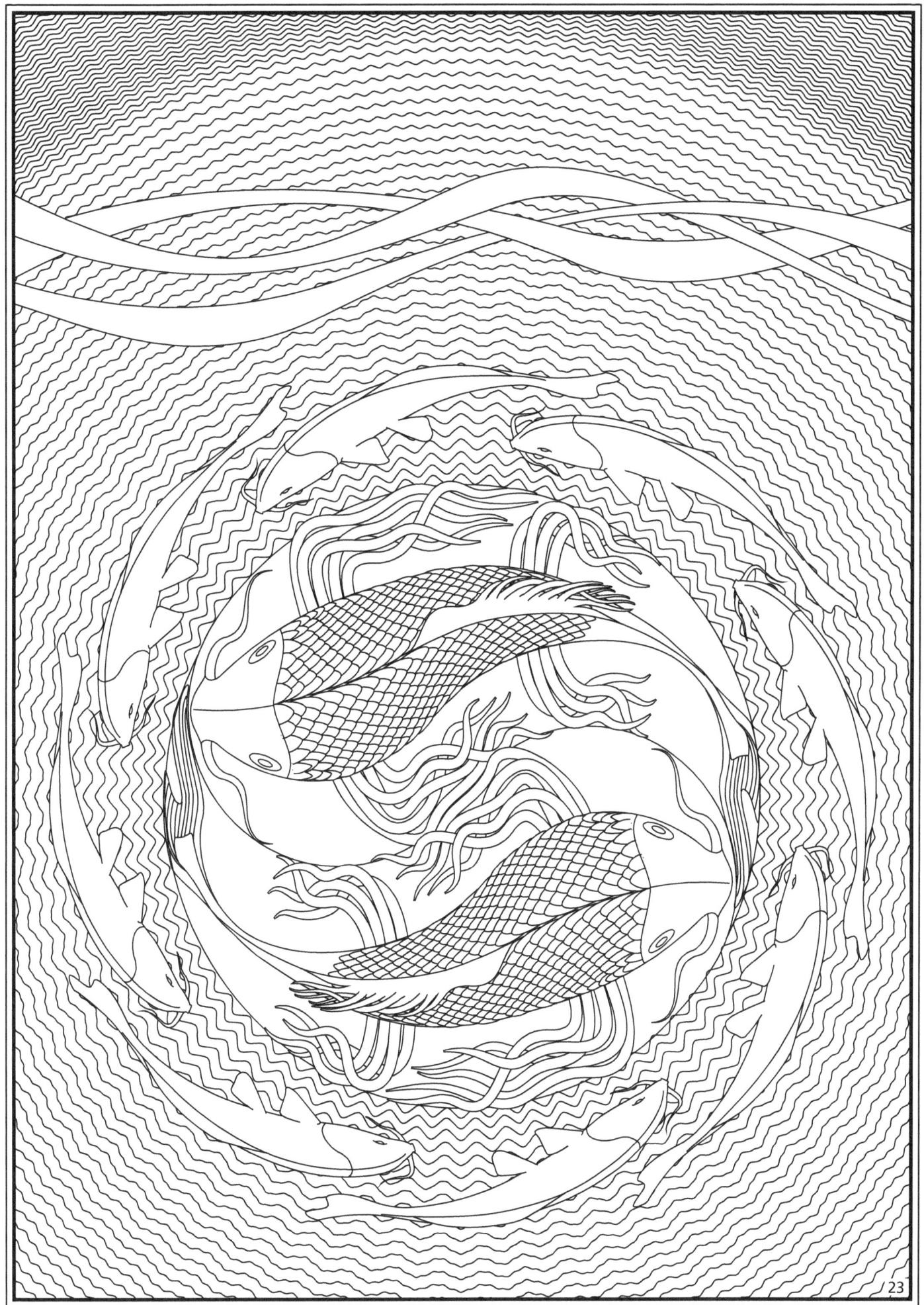

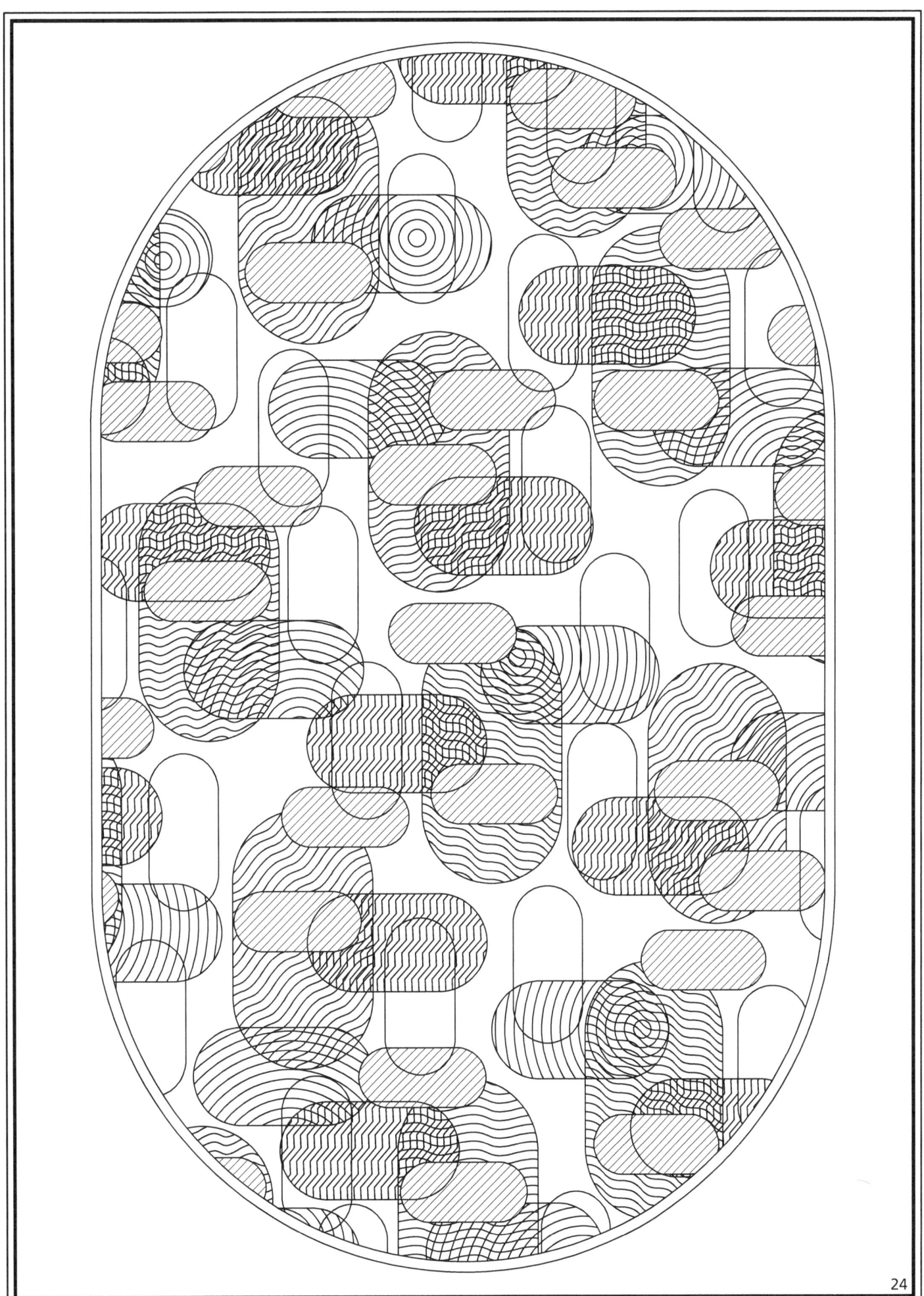

24

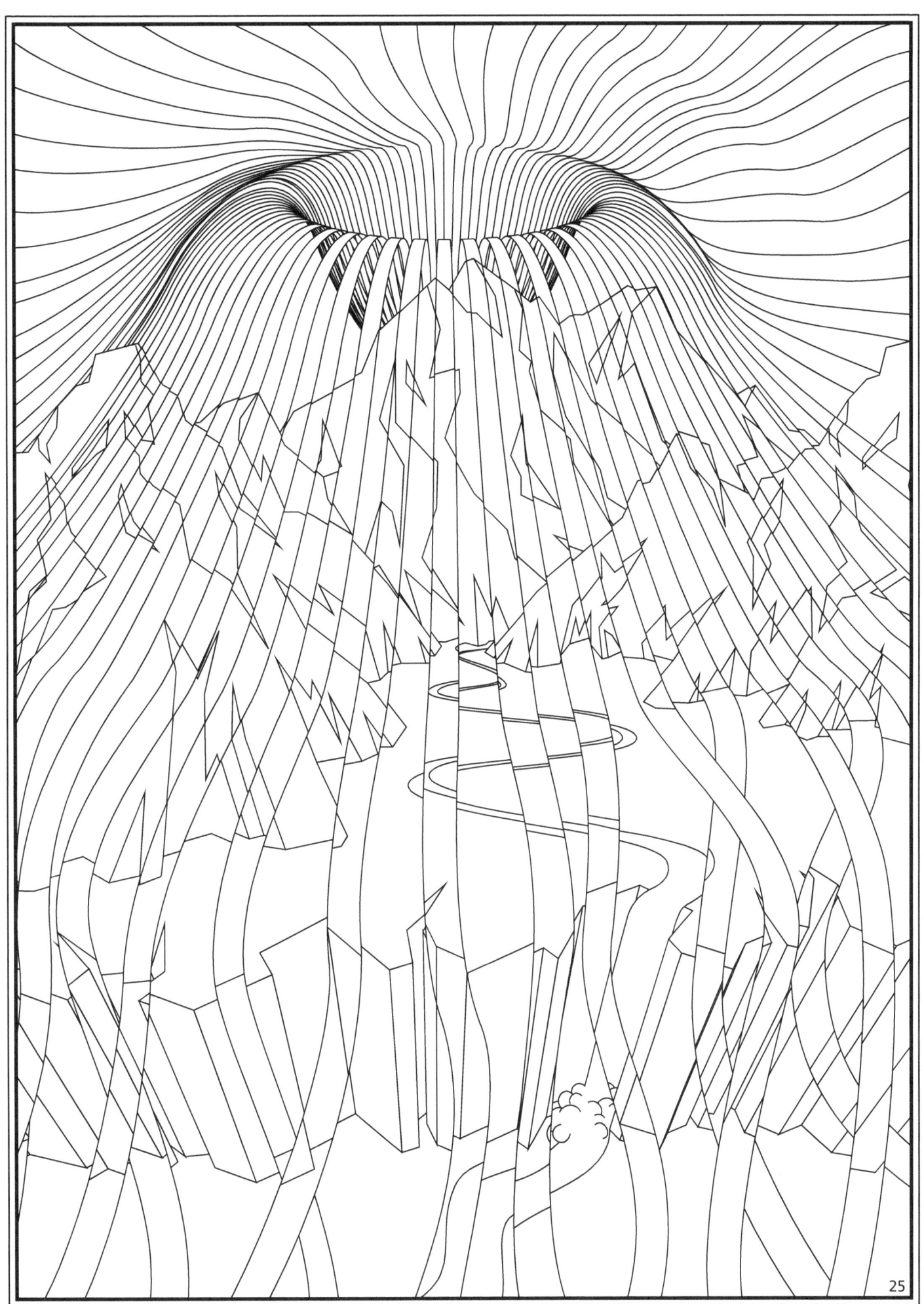

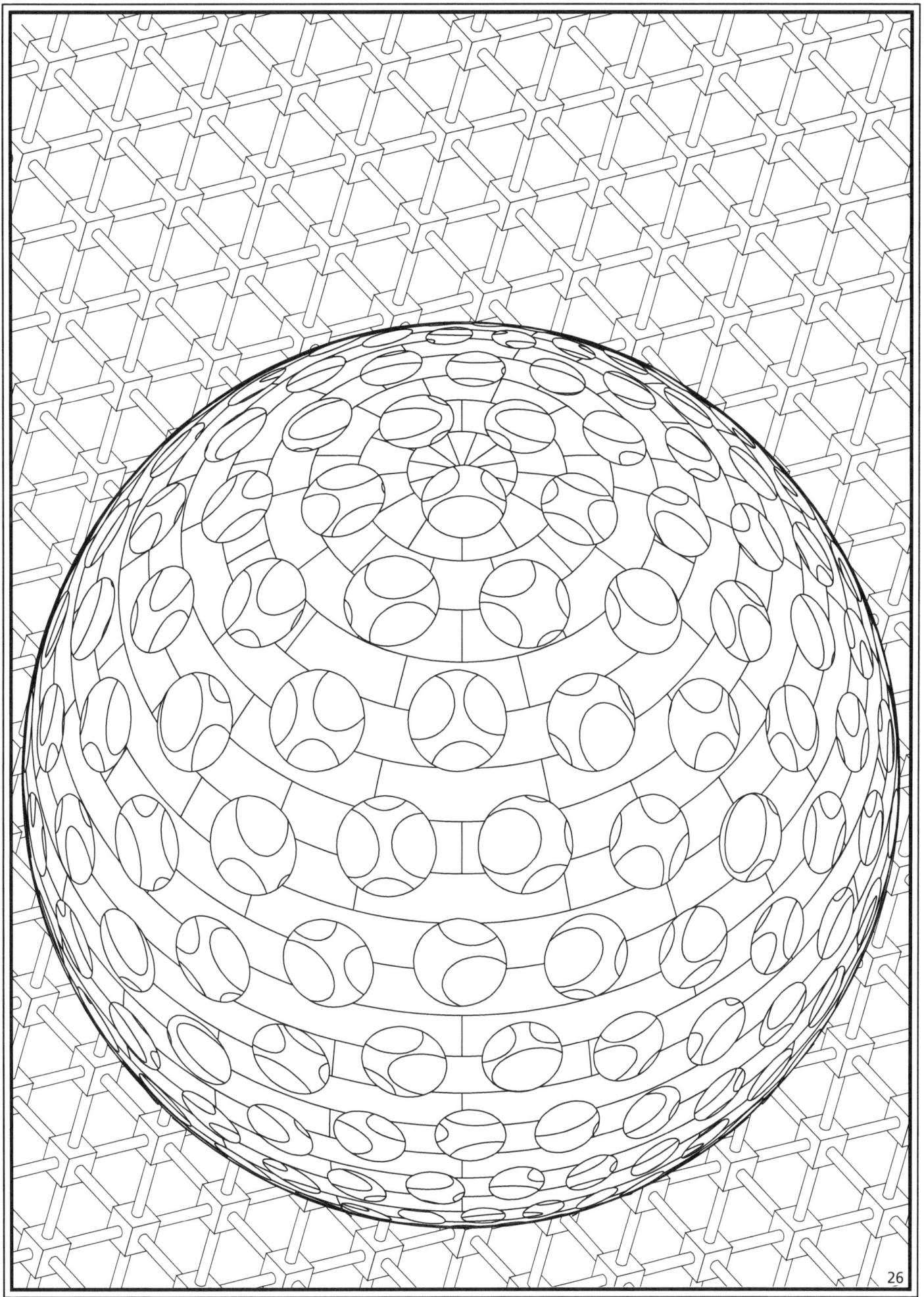

26

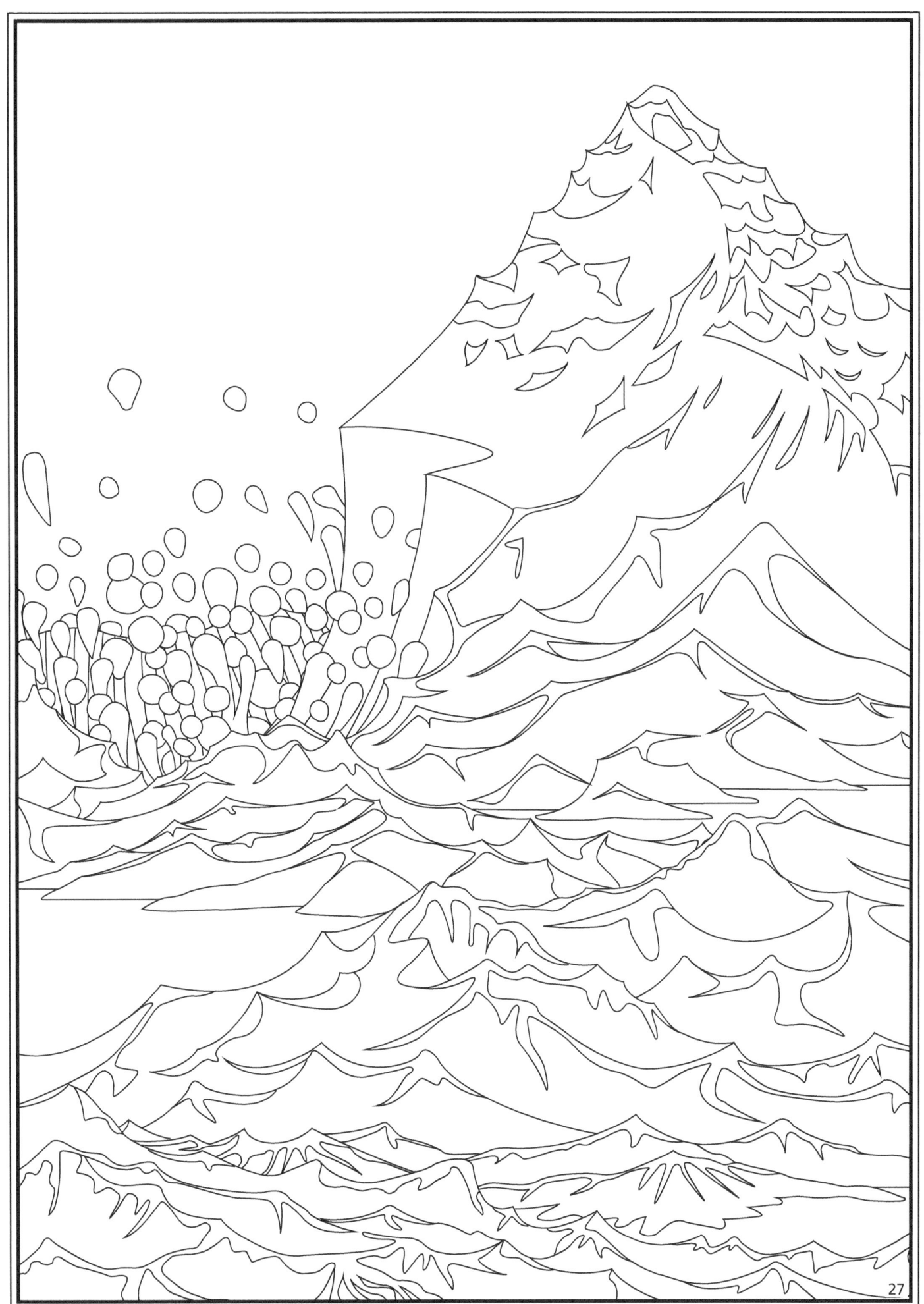

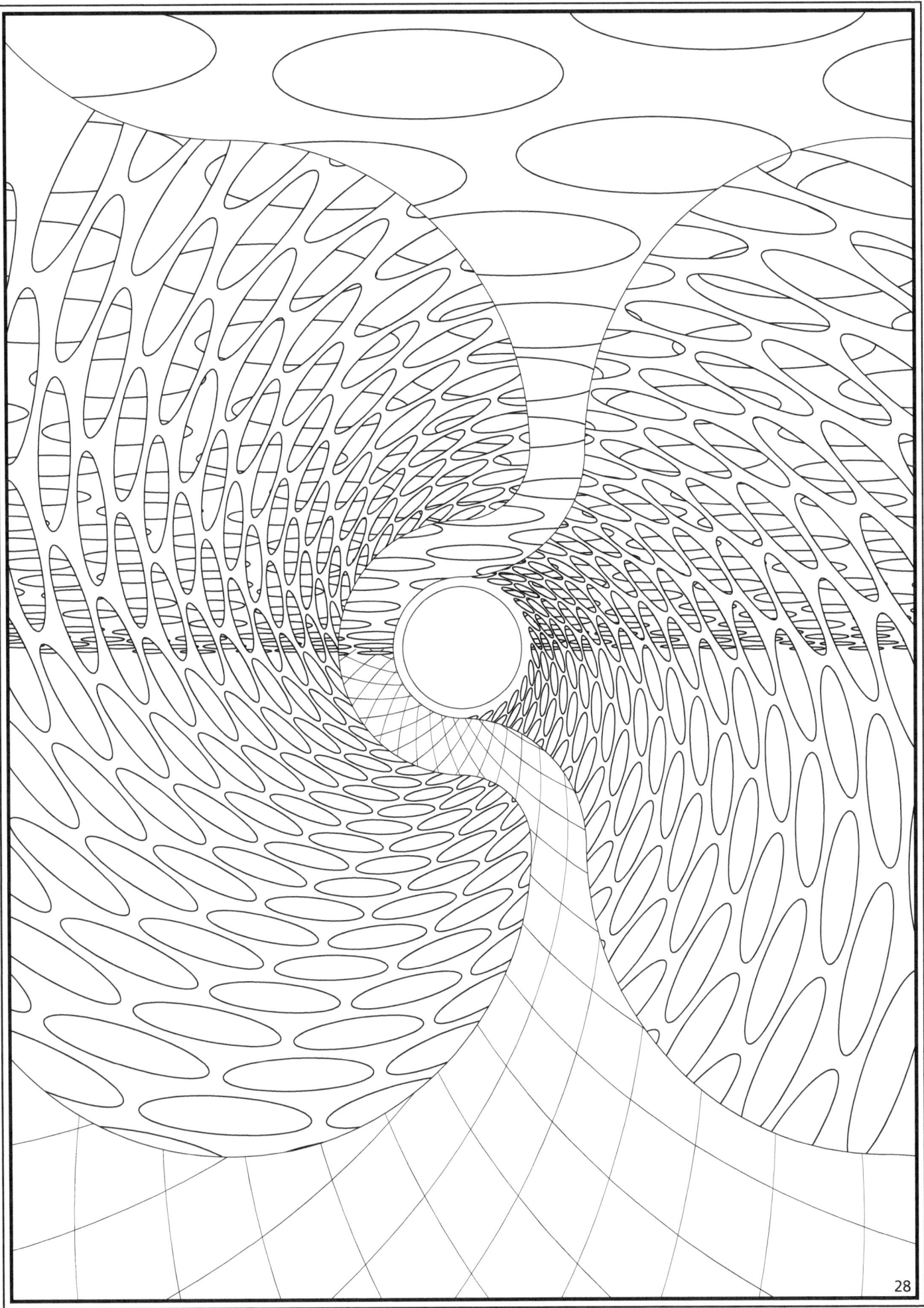

28

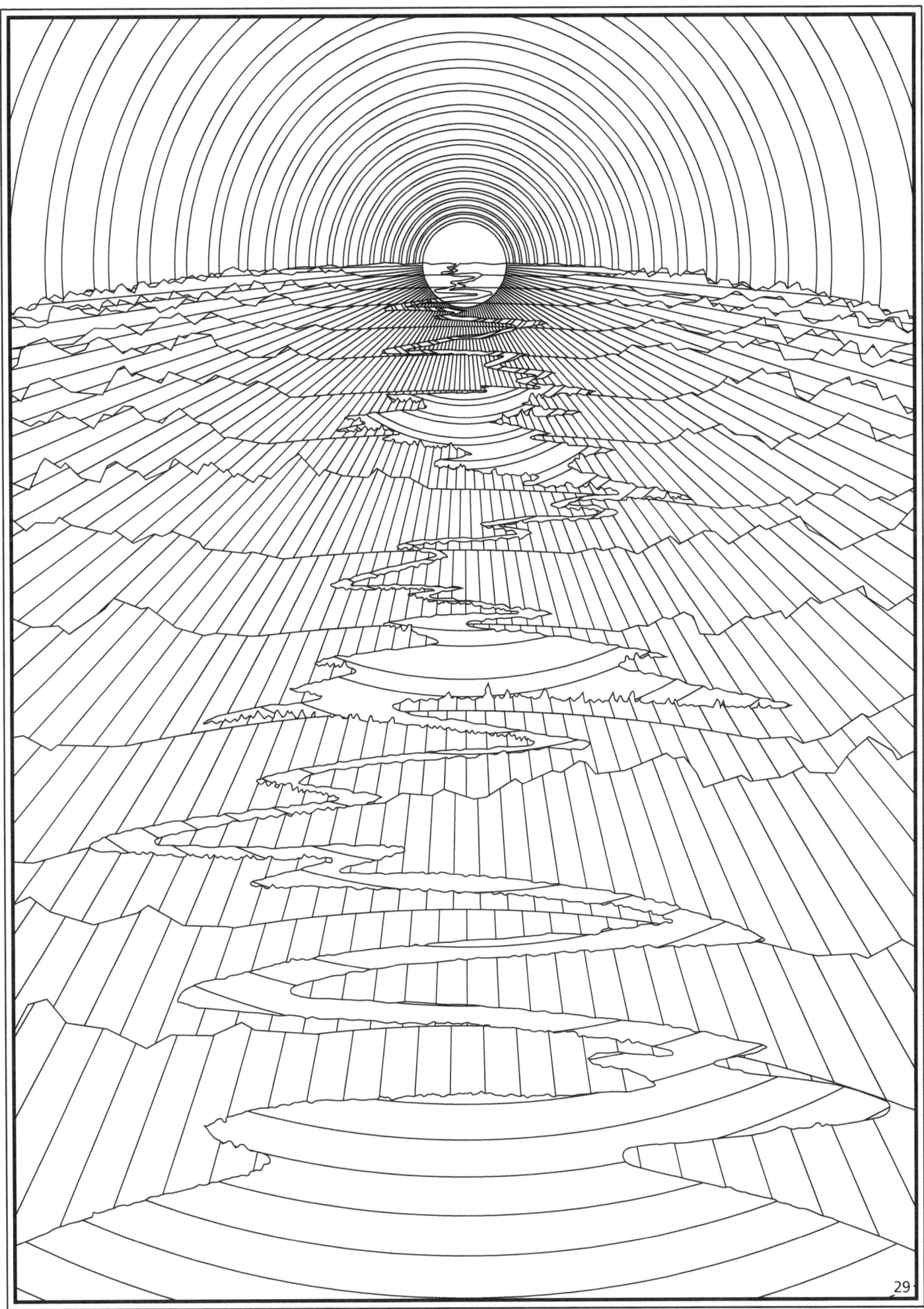

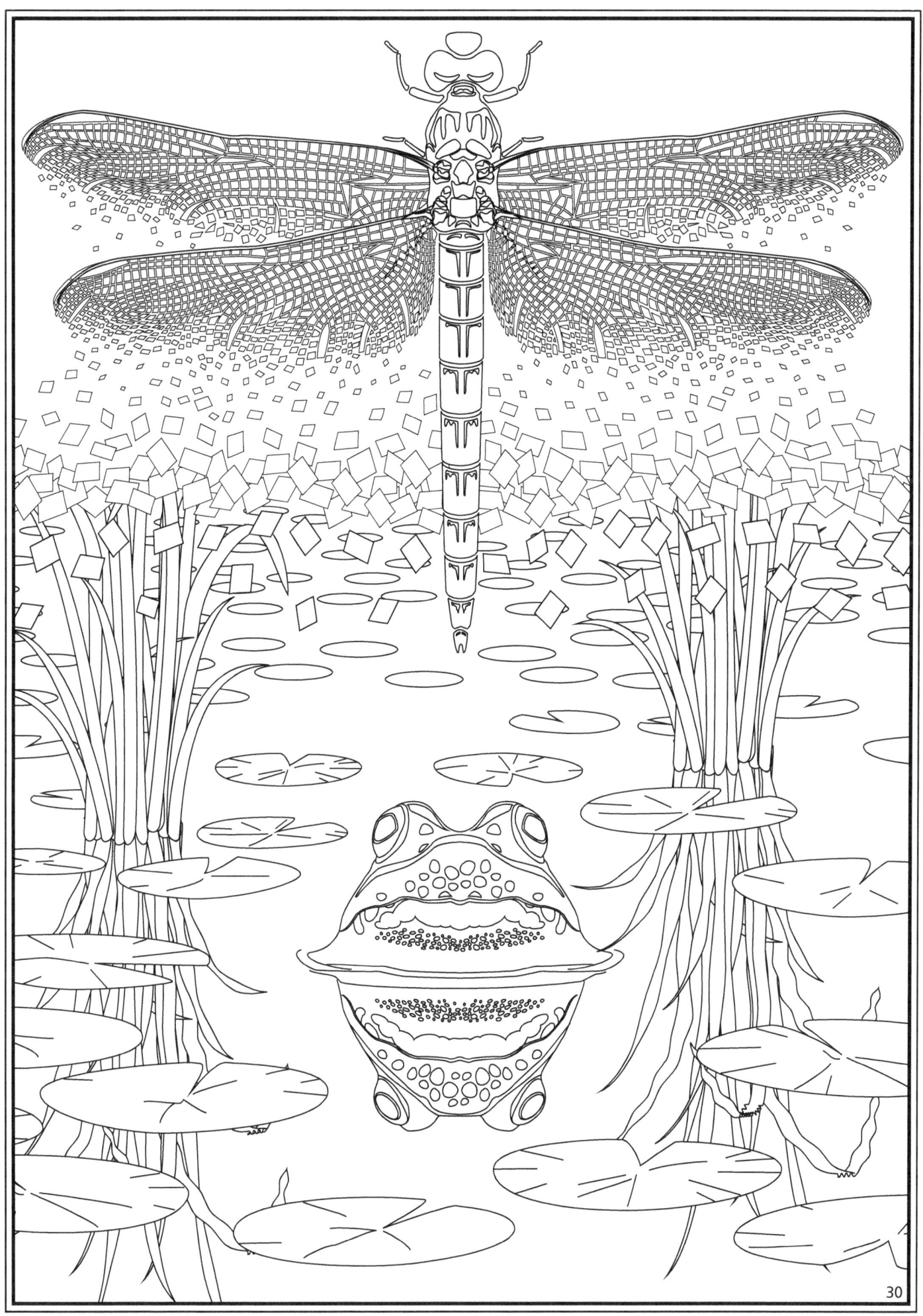

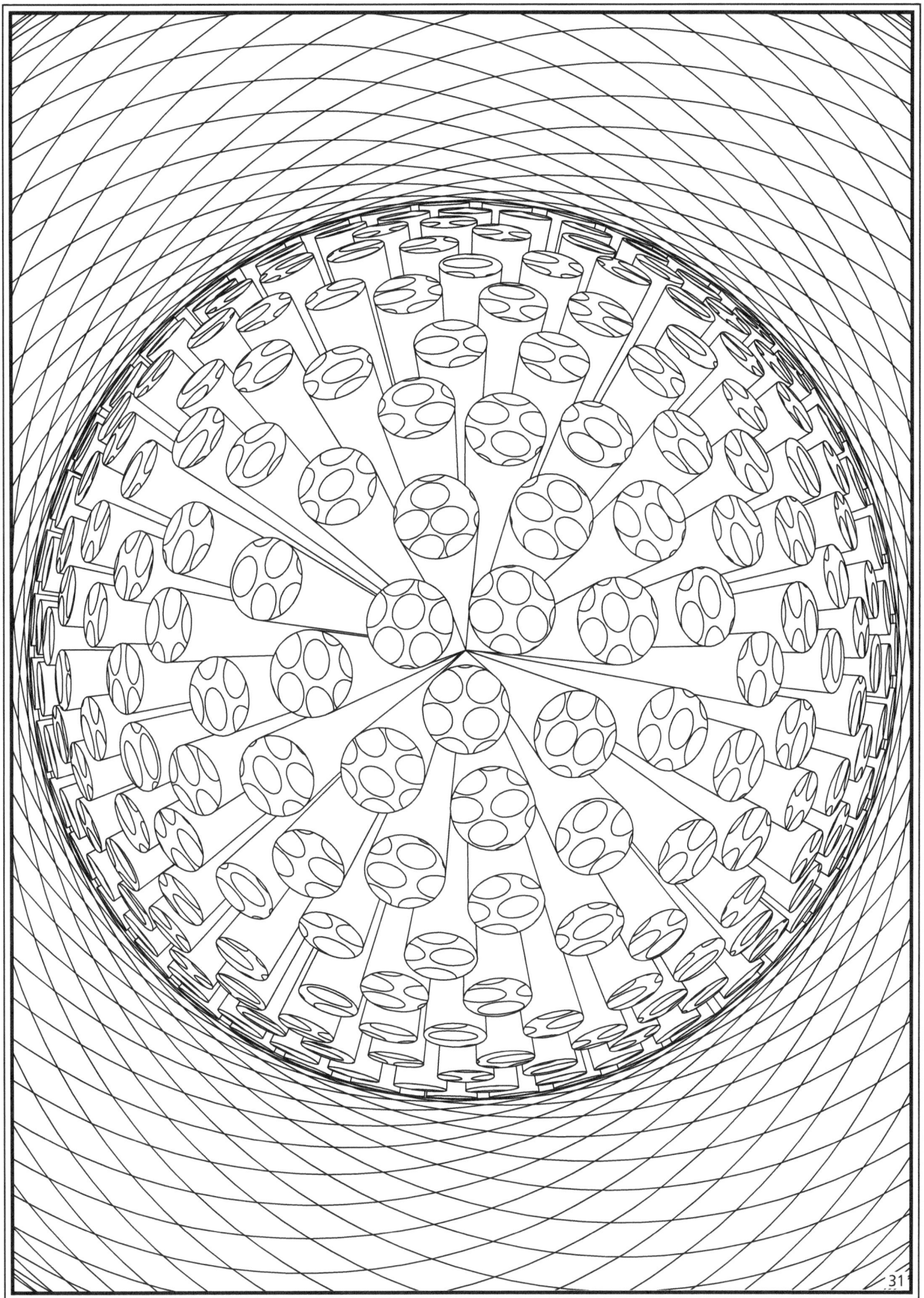

31

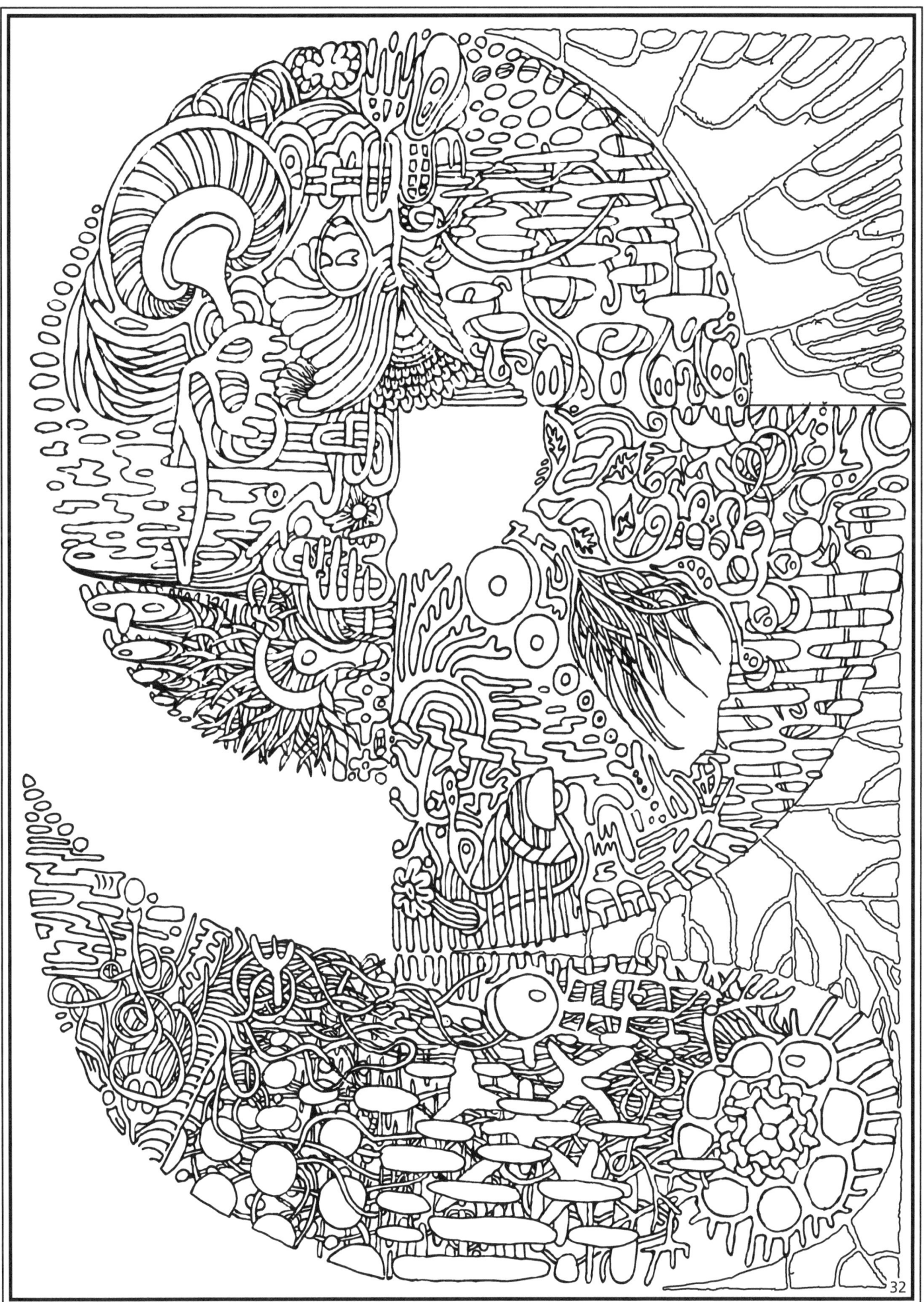

Section II
Second Chance

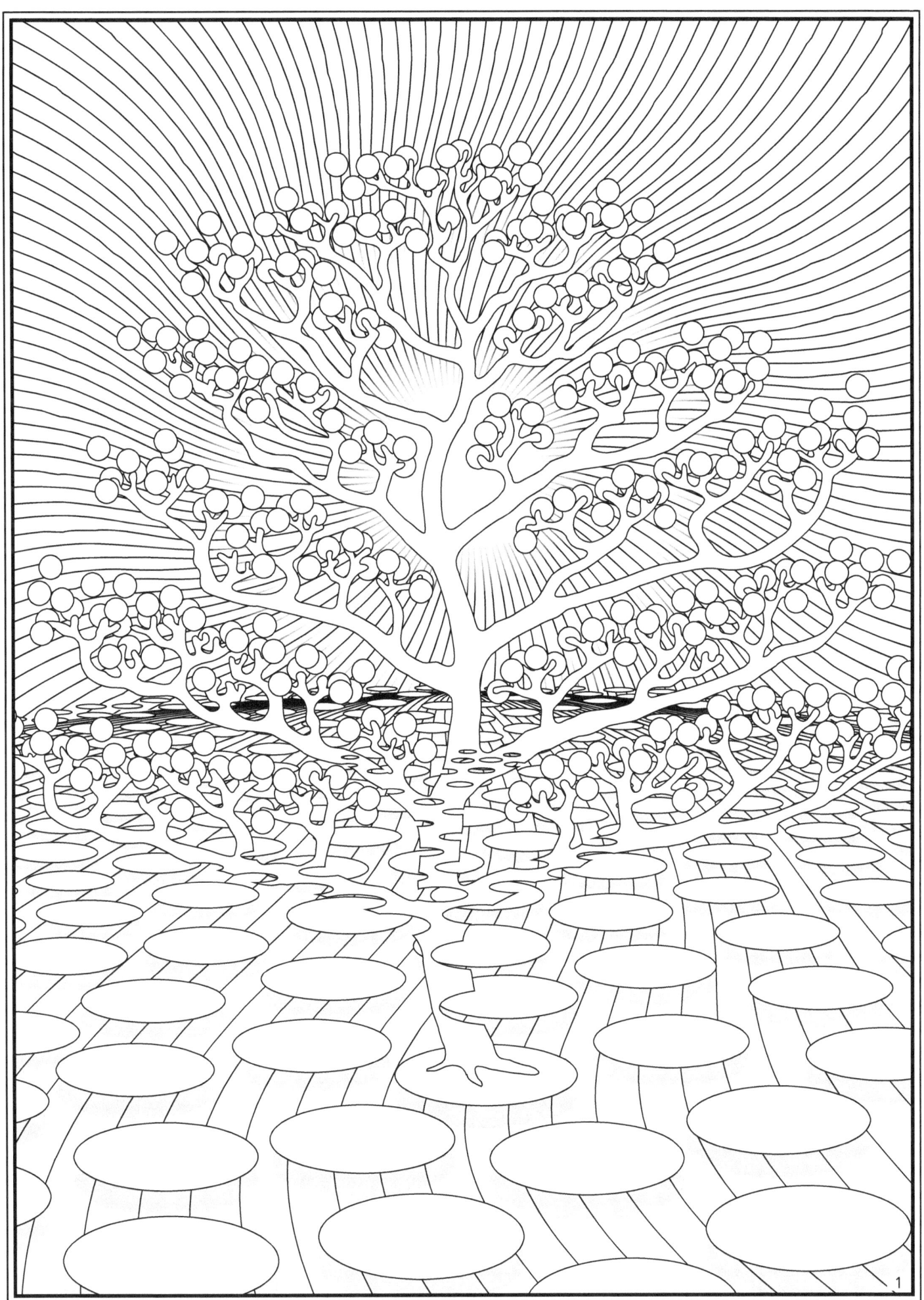

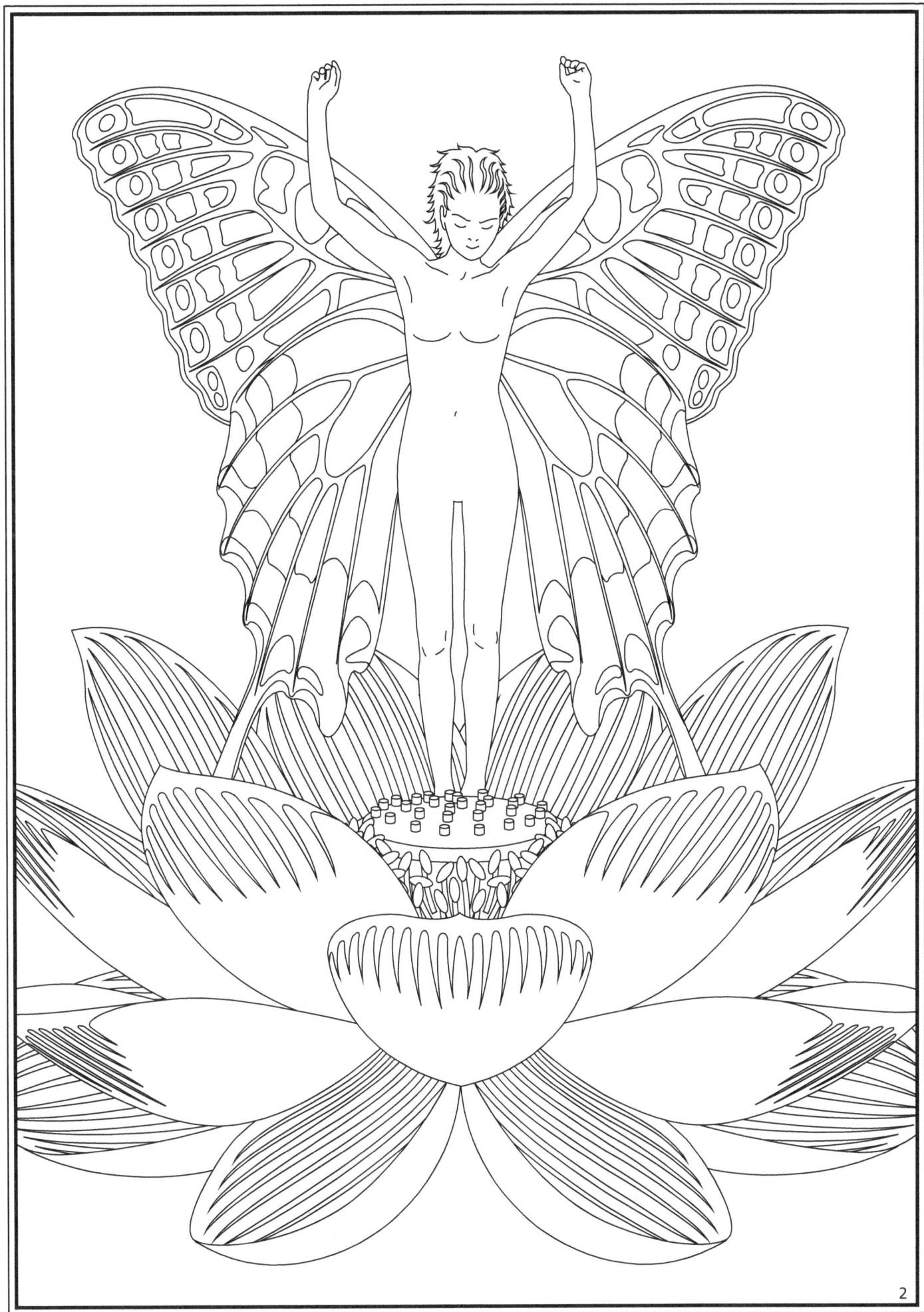

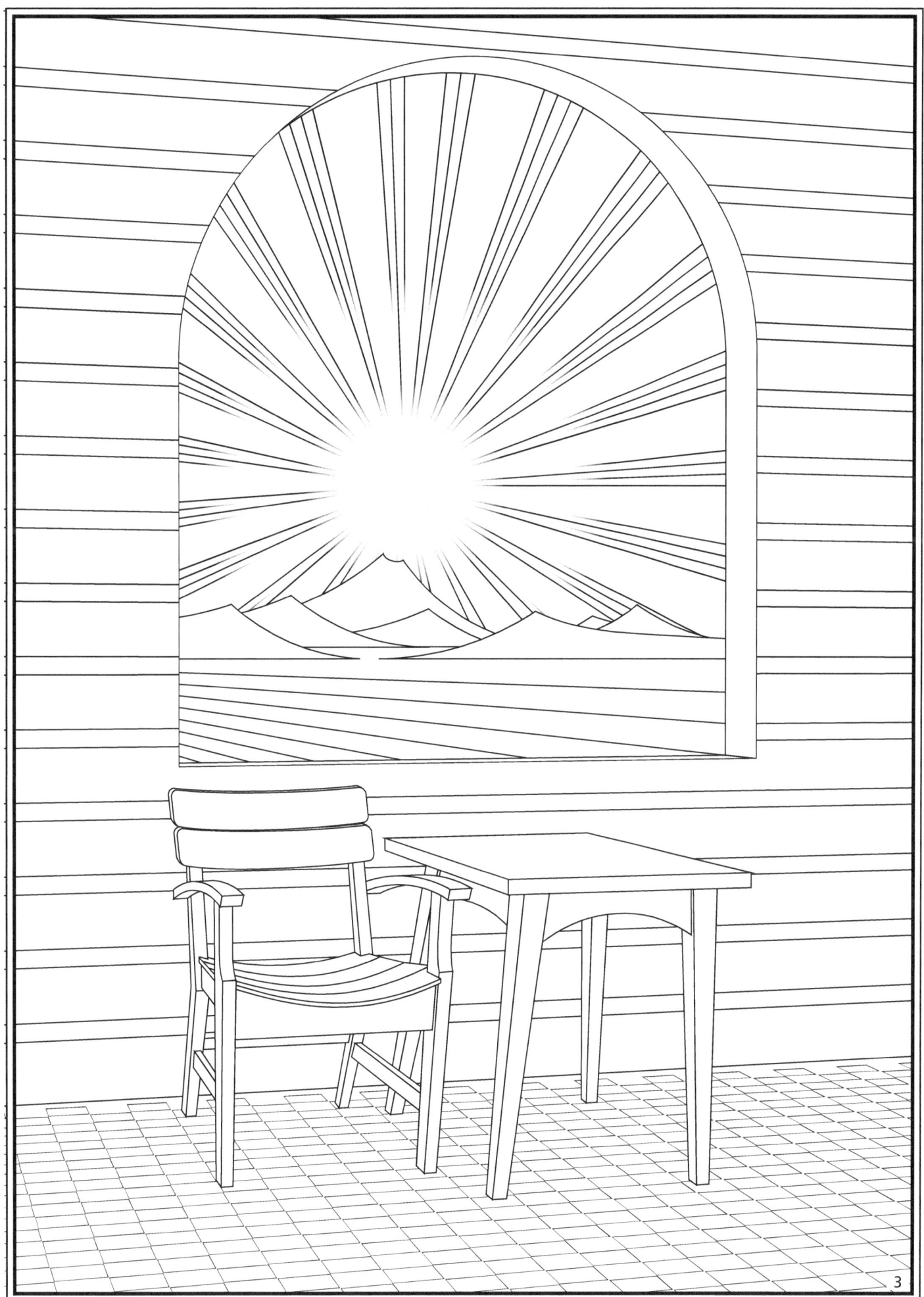

3

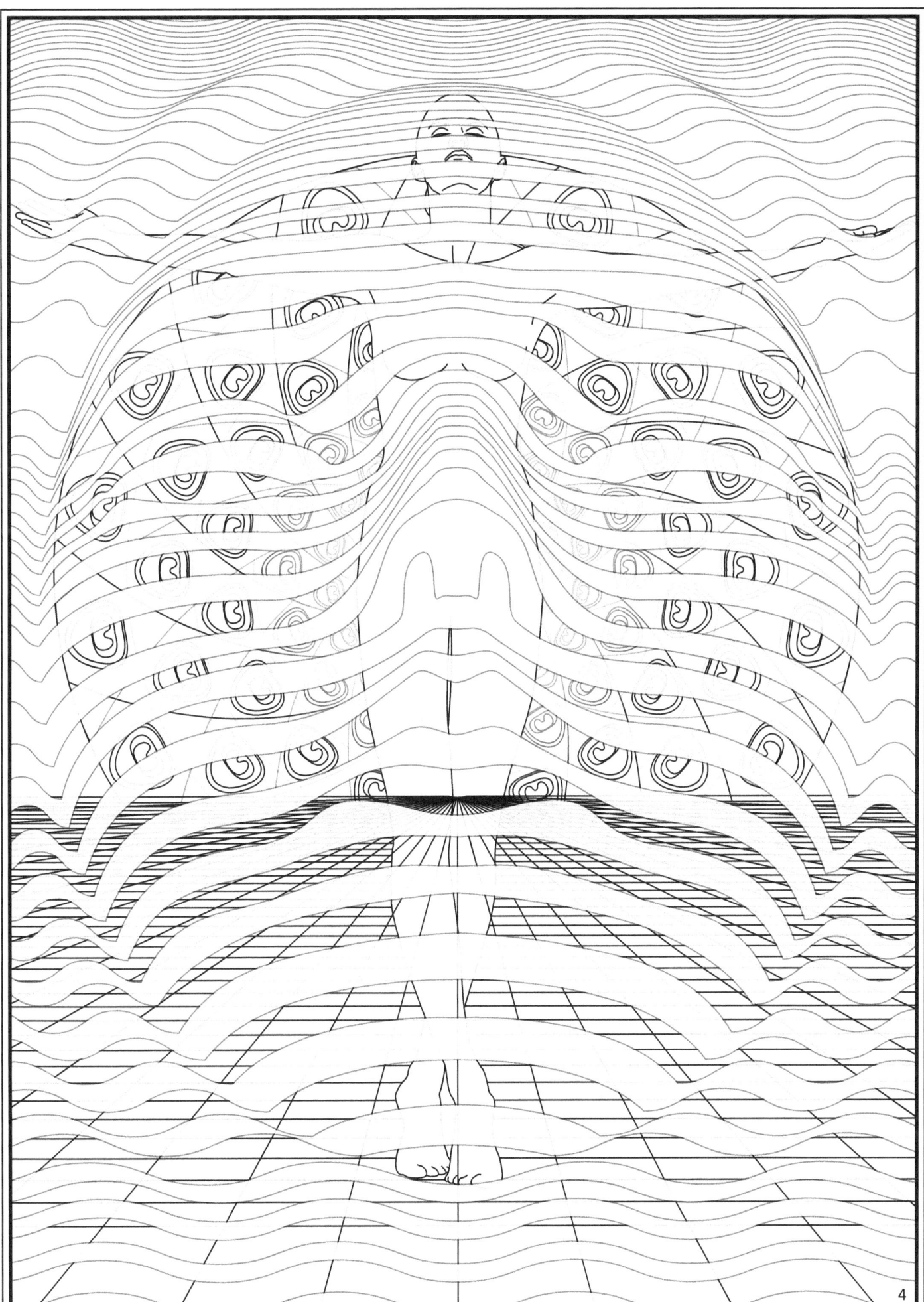

4

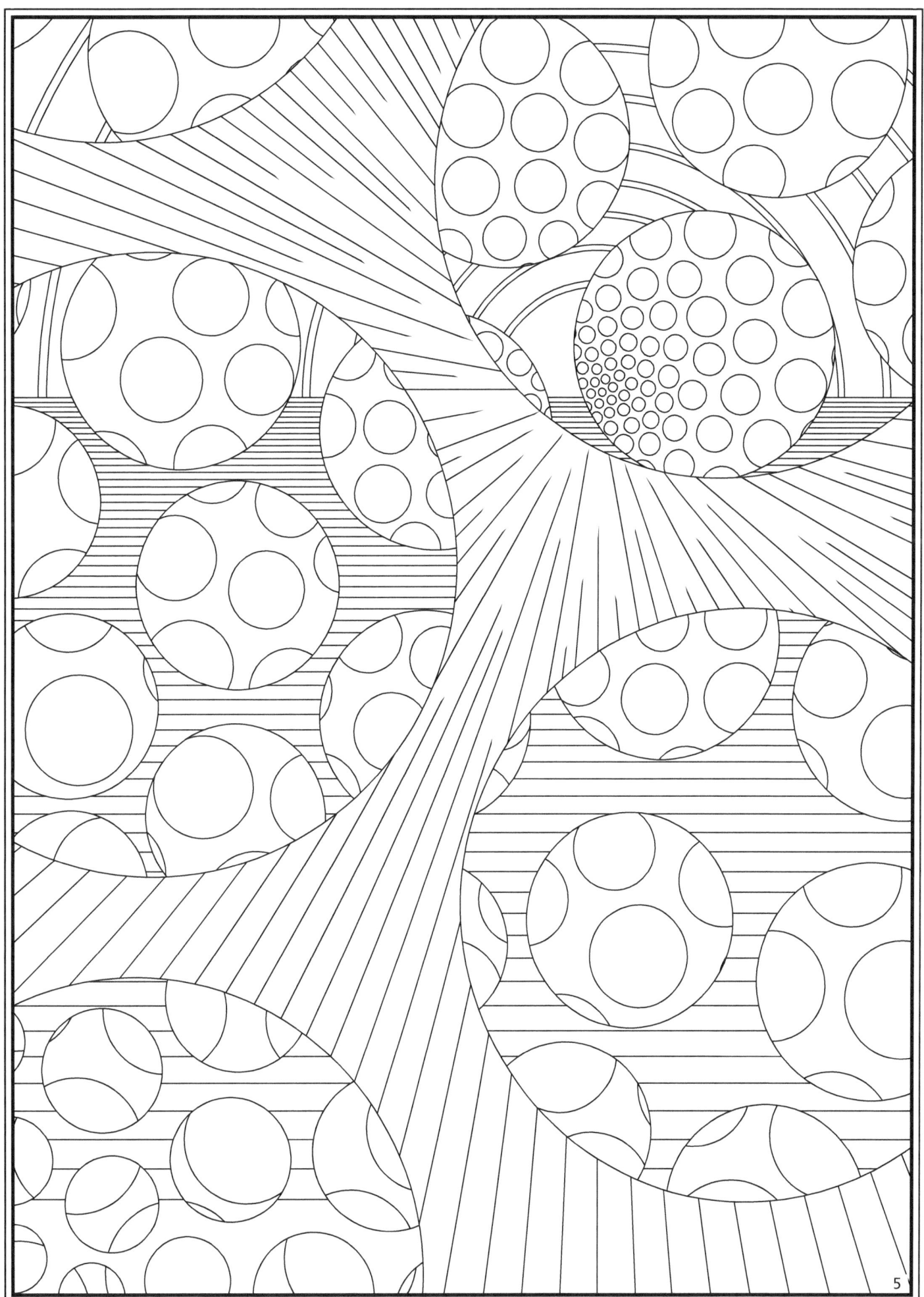

5

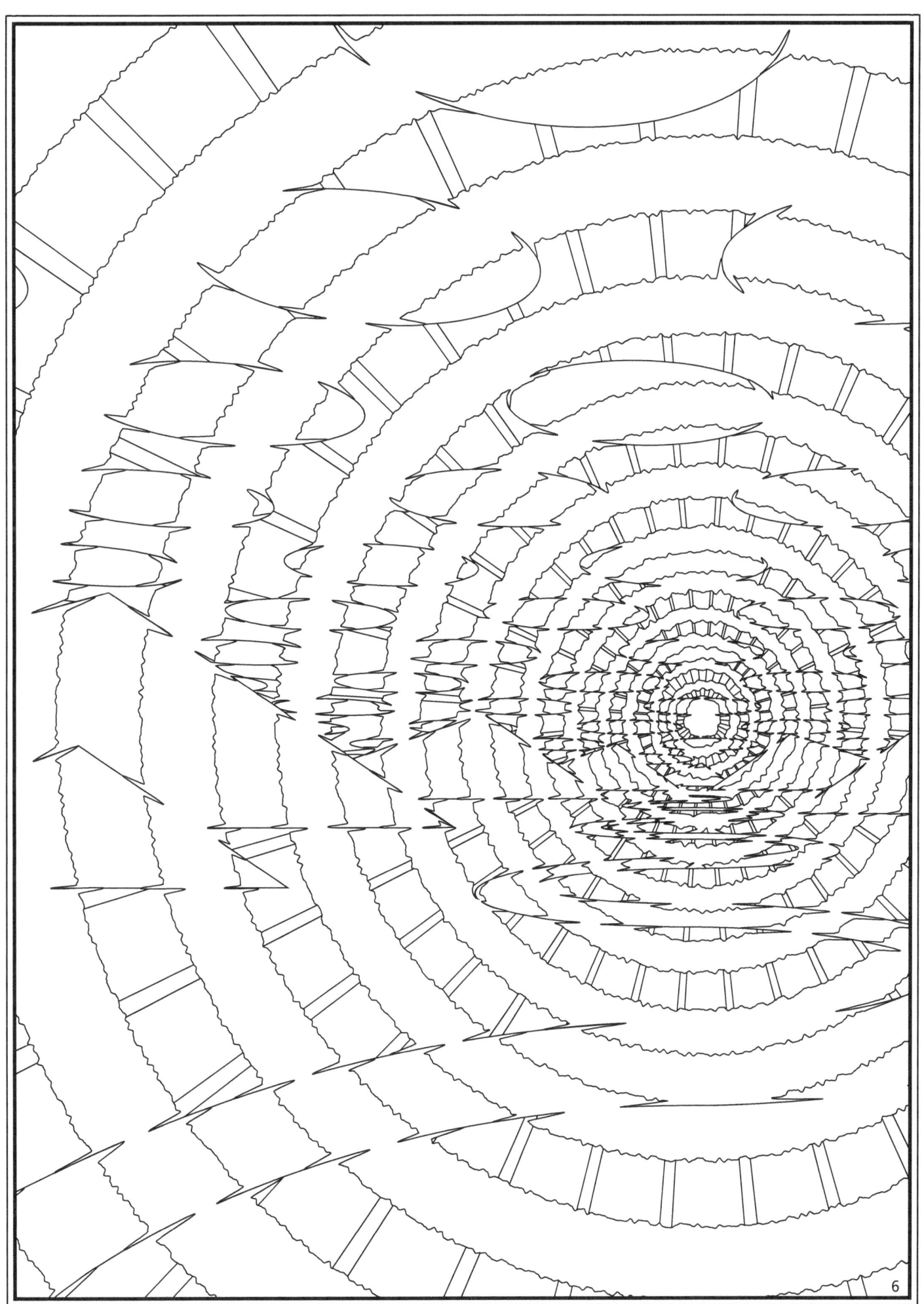

6

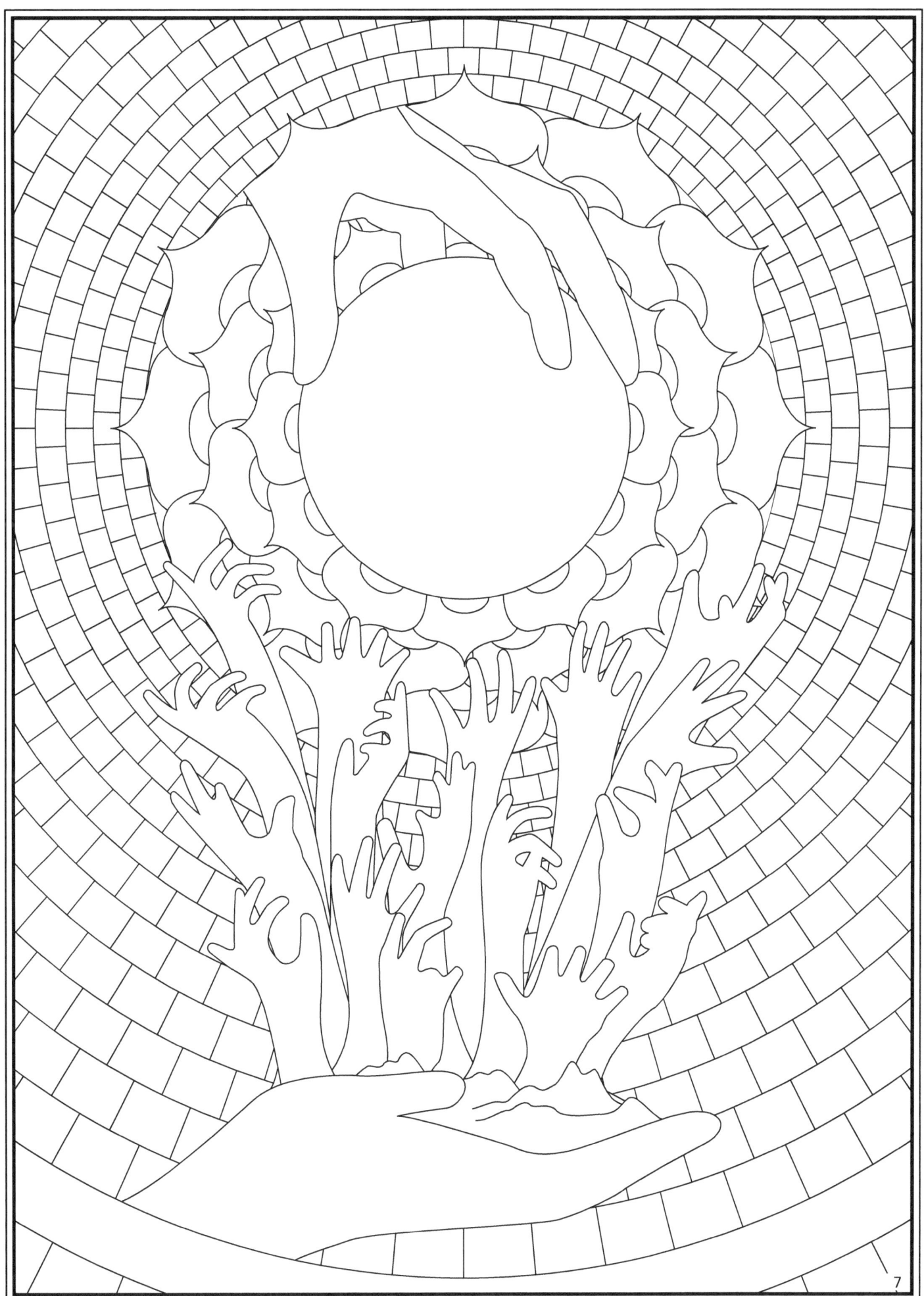

7

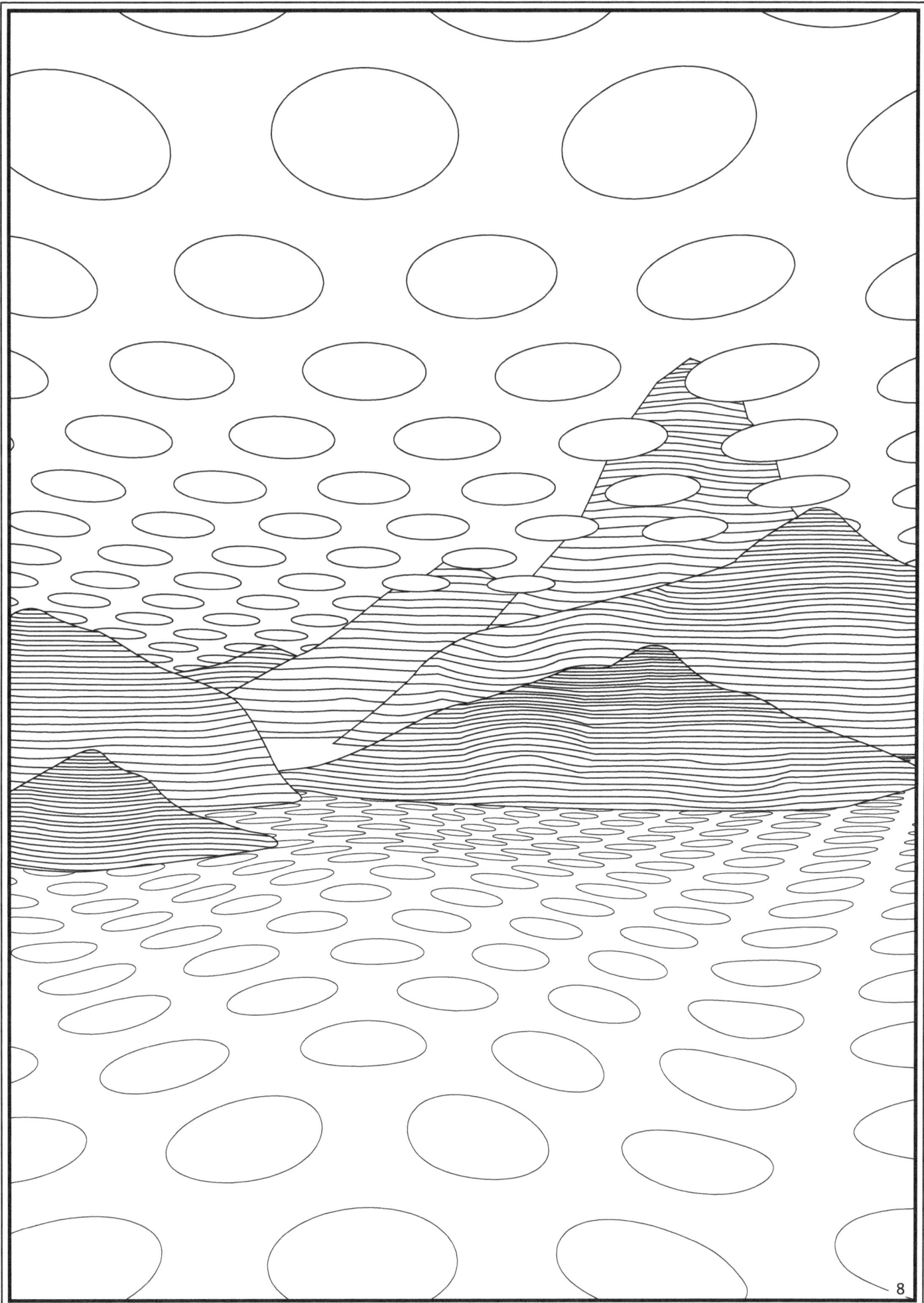

8

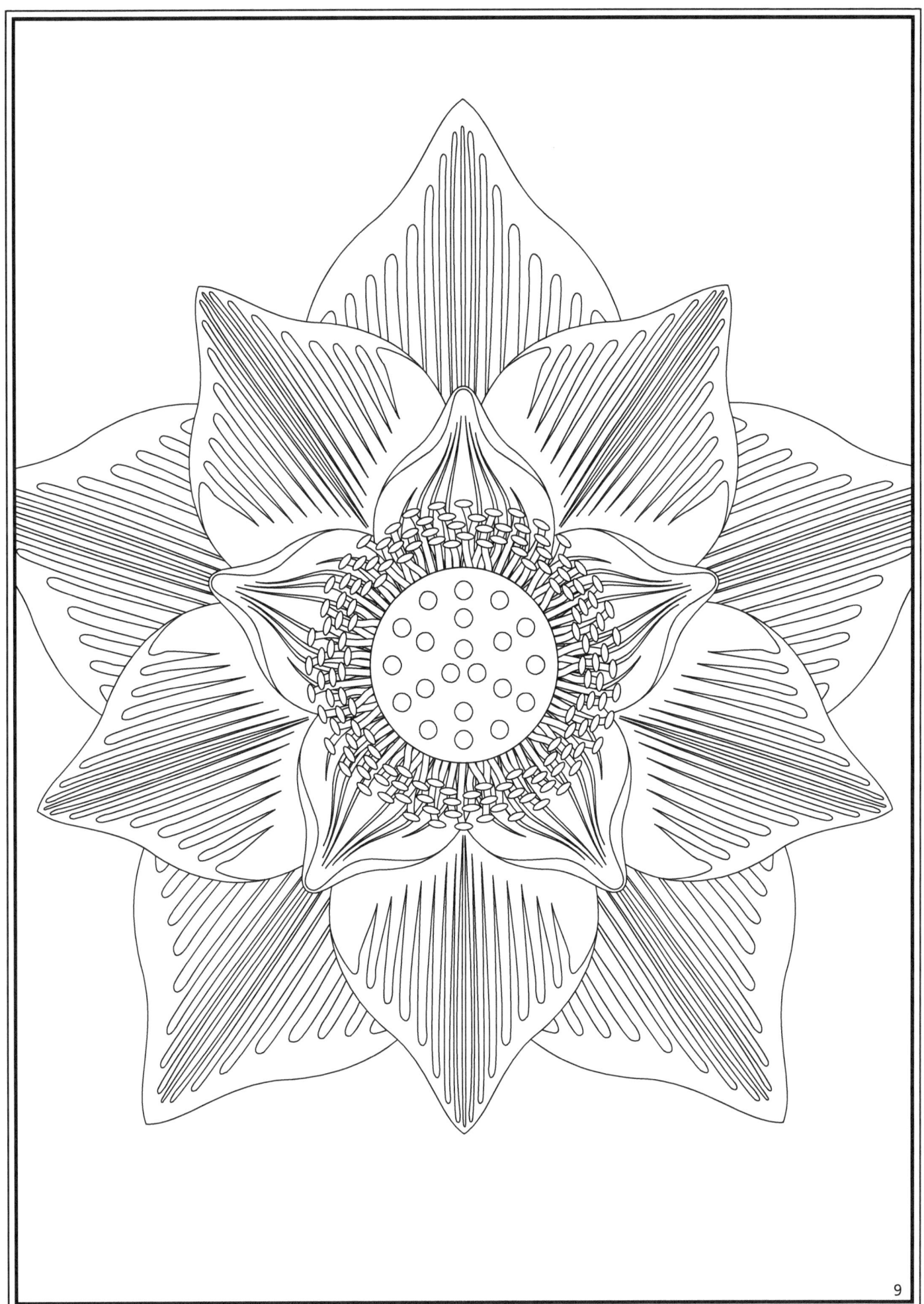

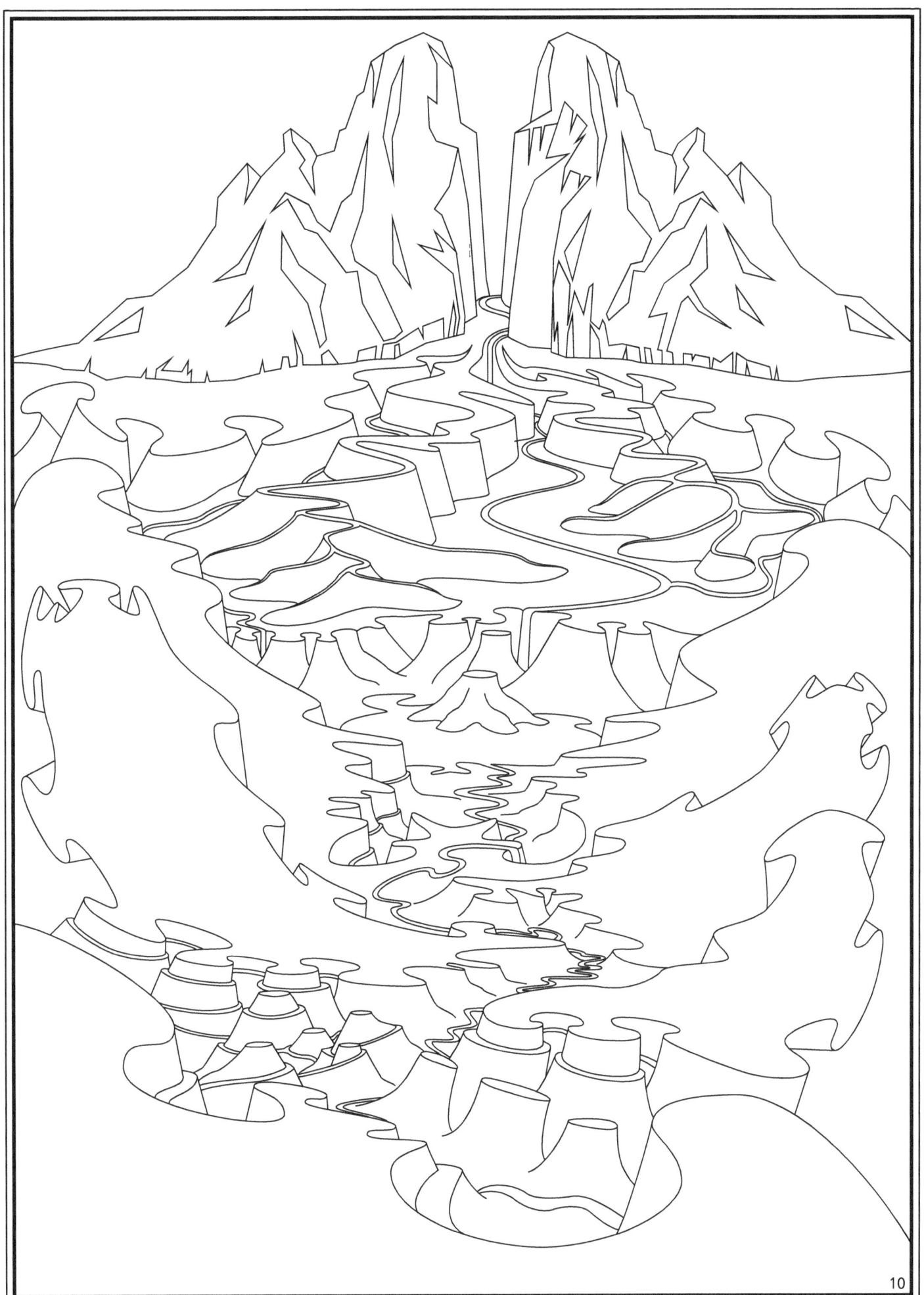

10

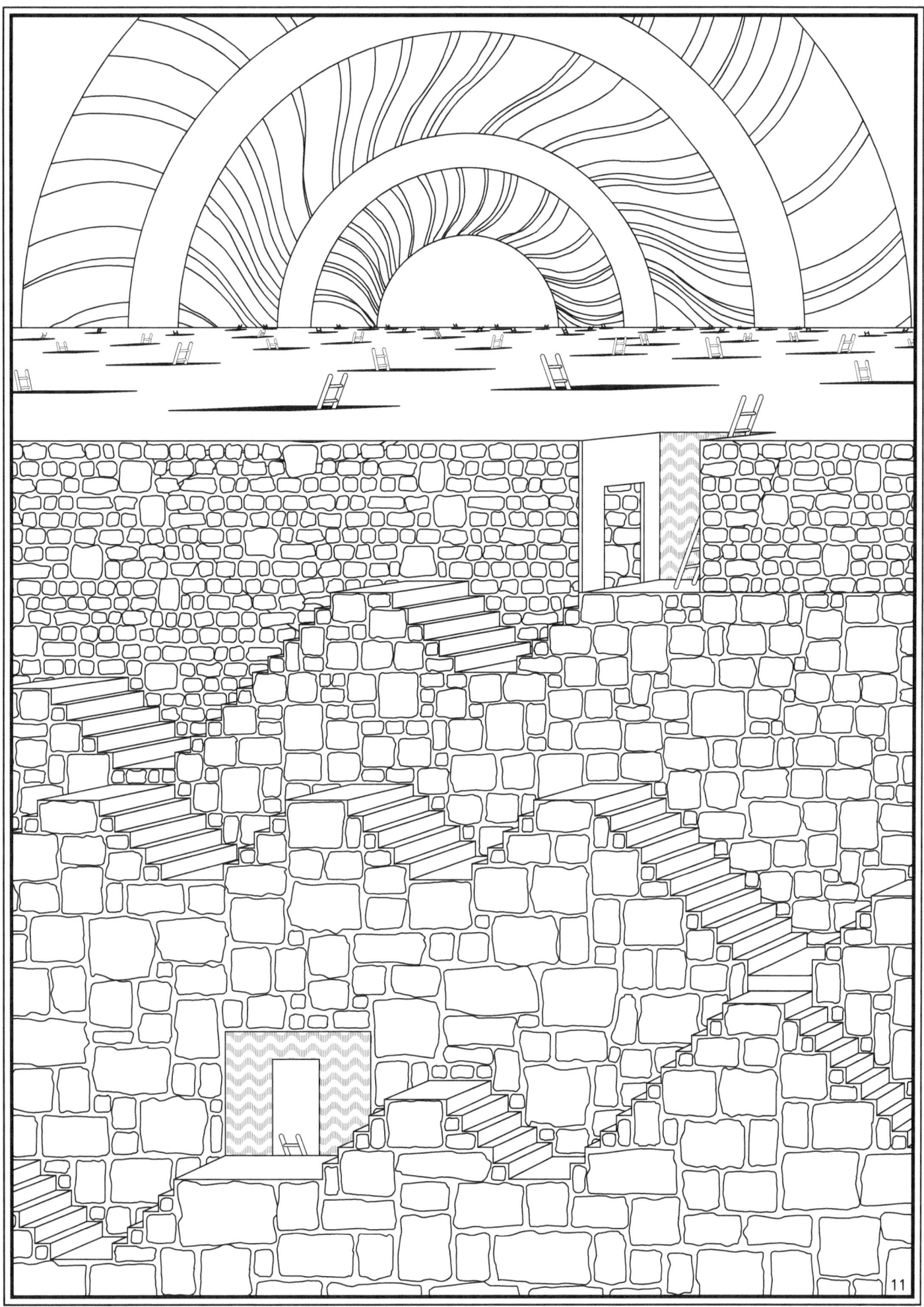

11

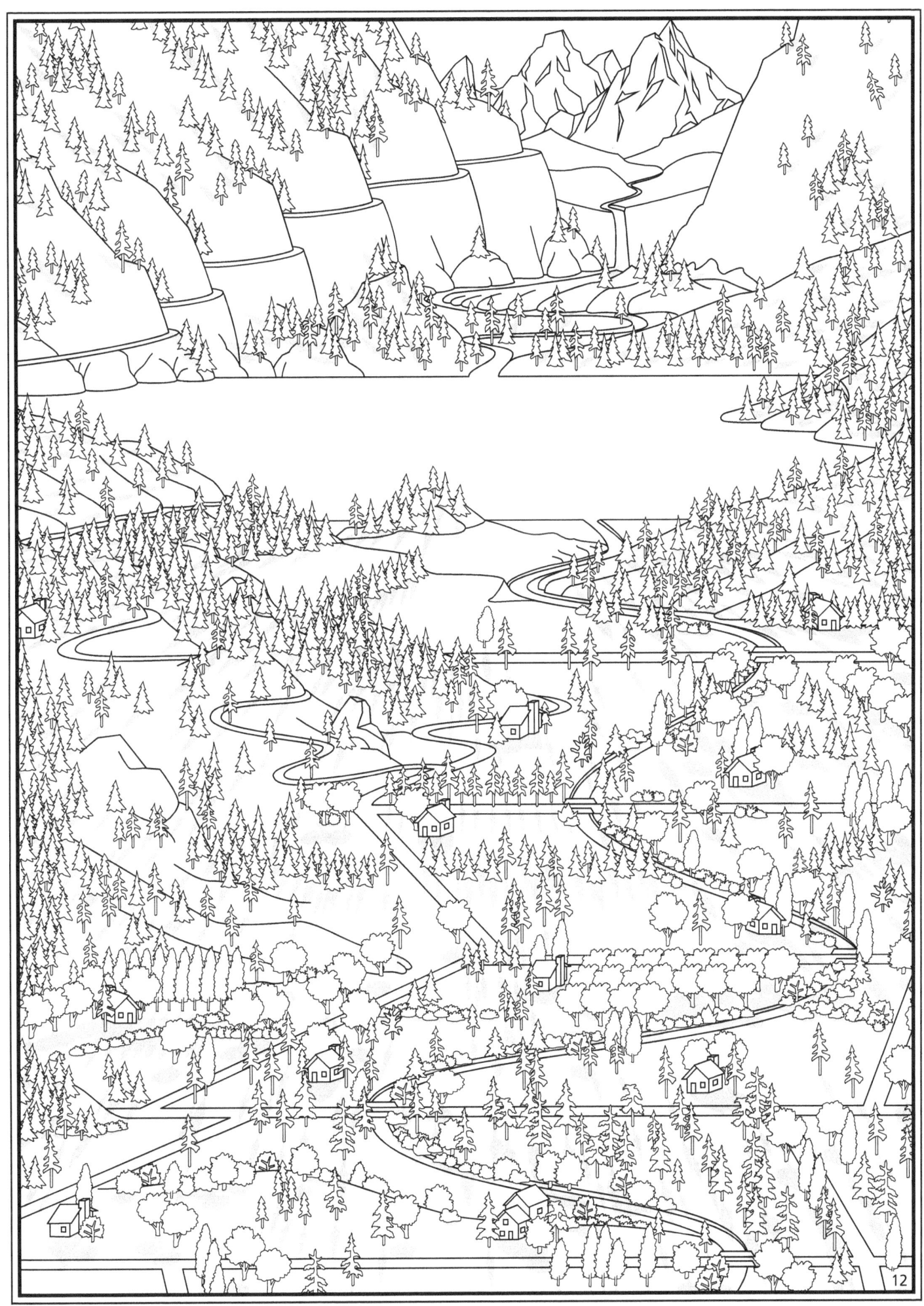

12

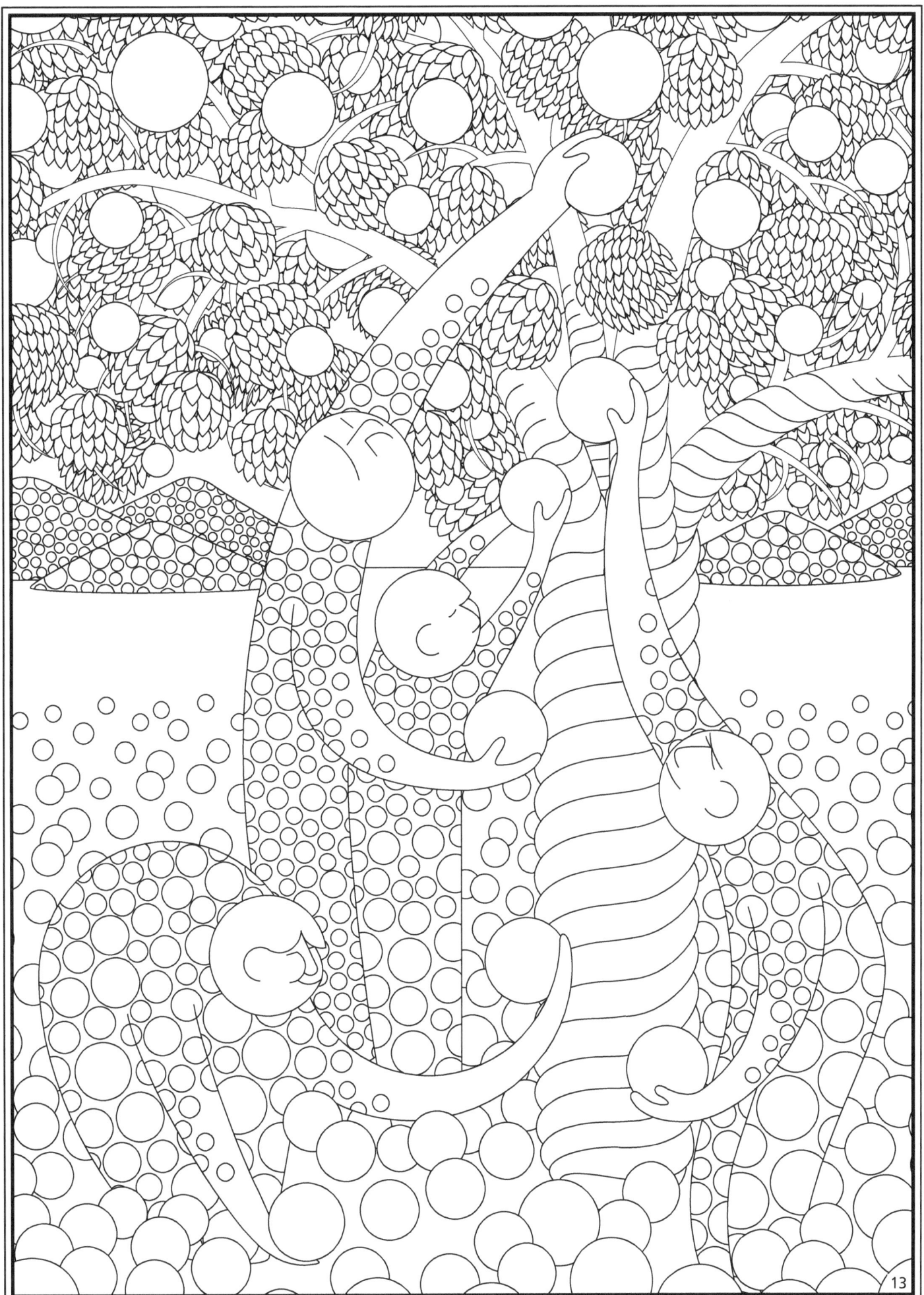

13

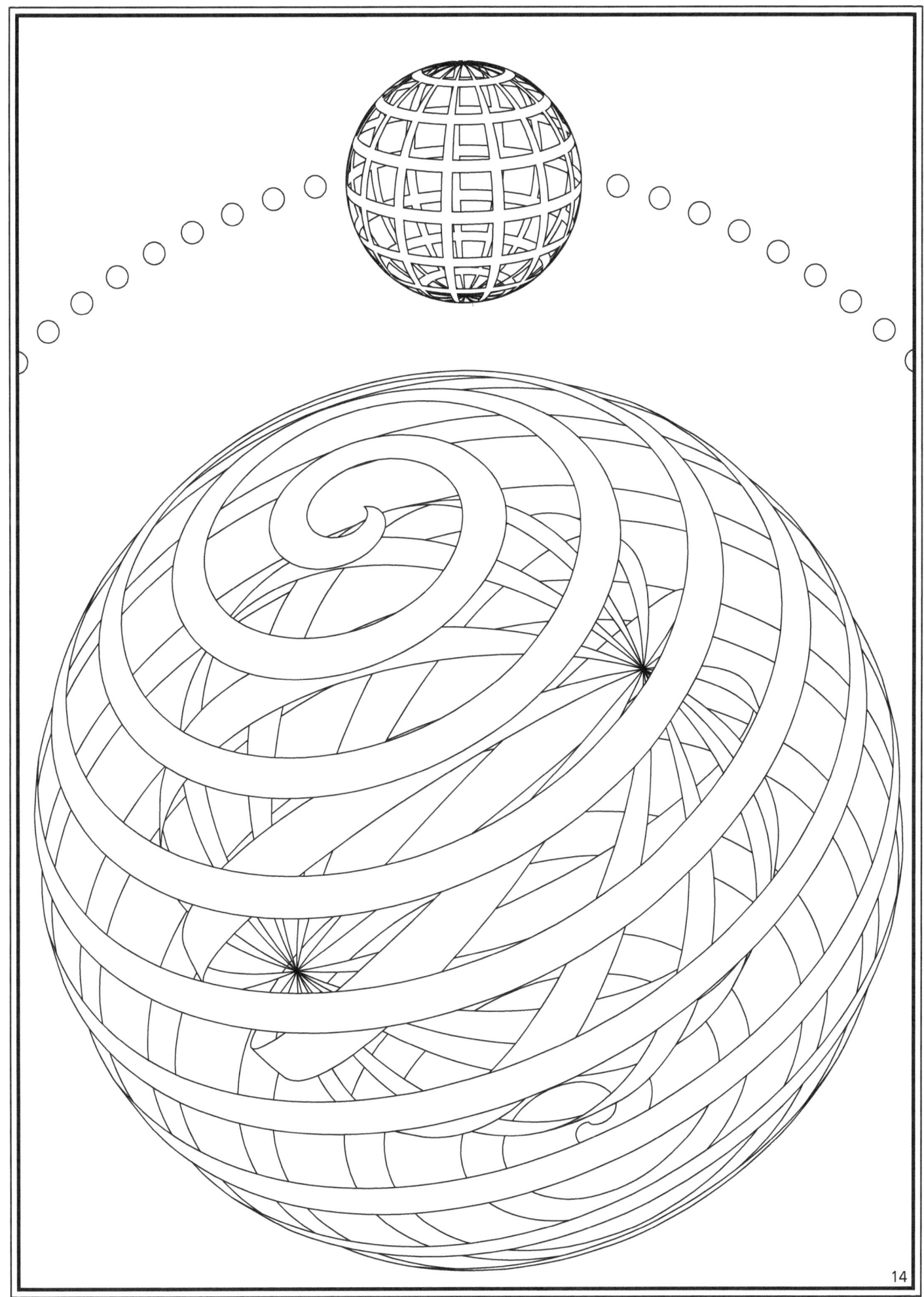

14

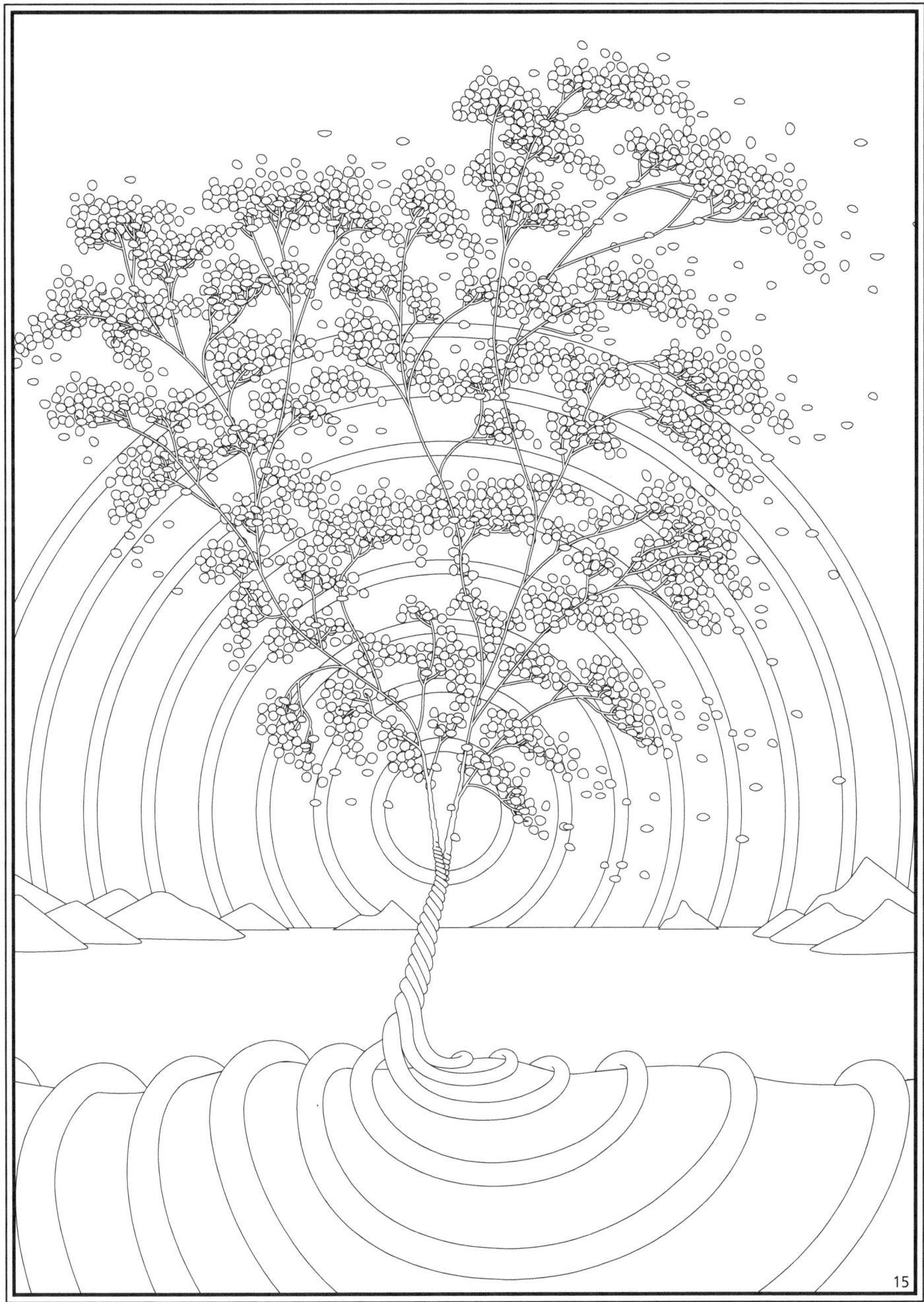

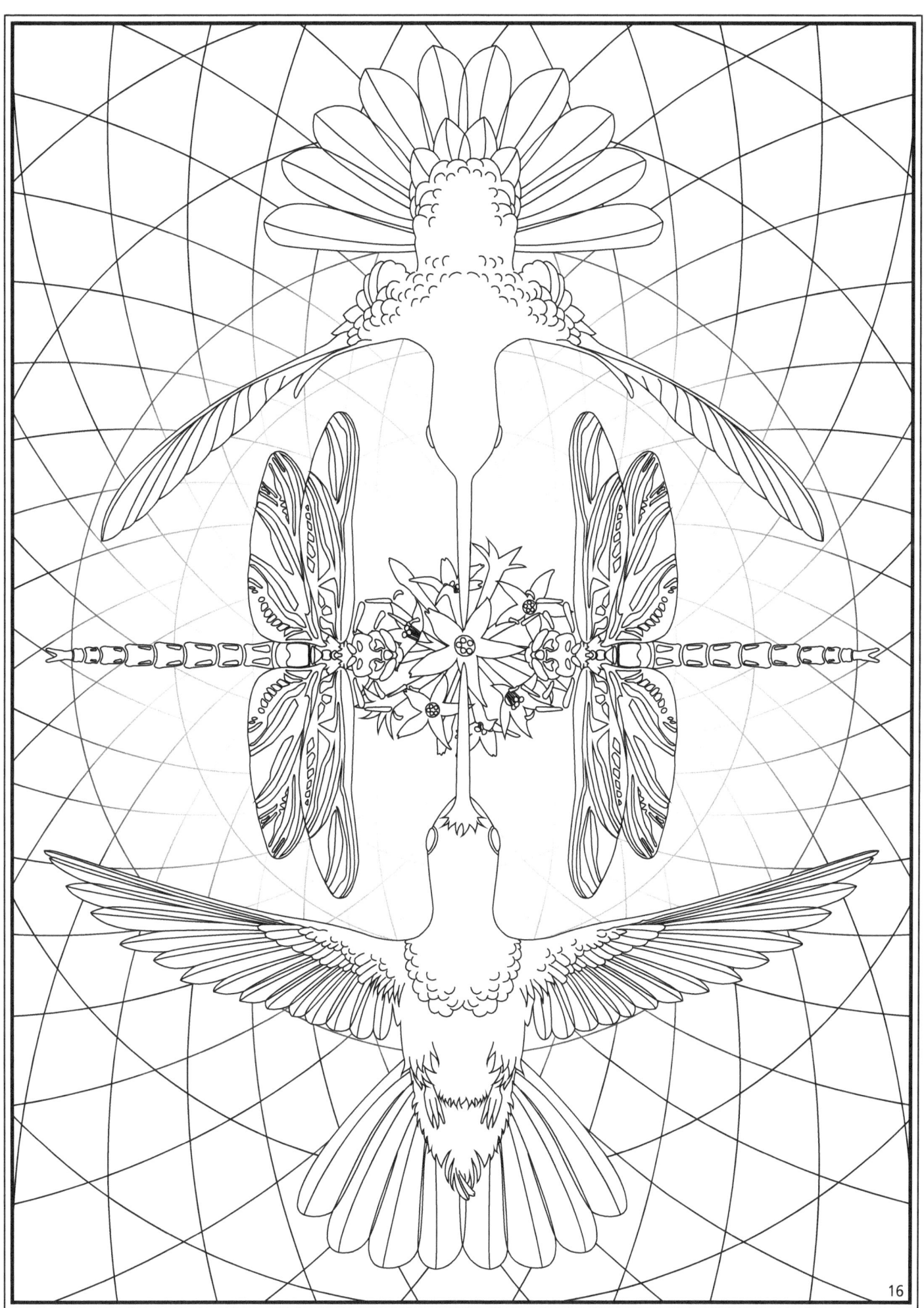

16

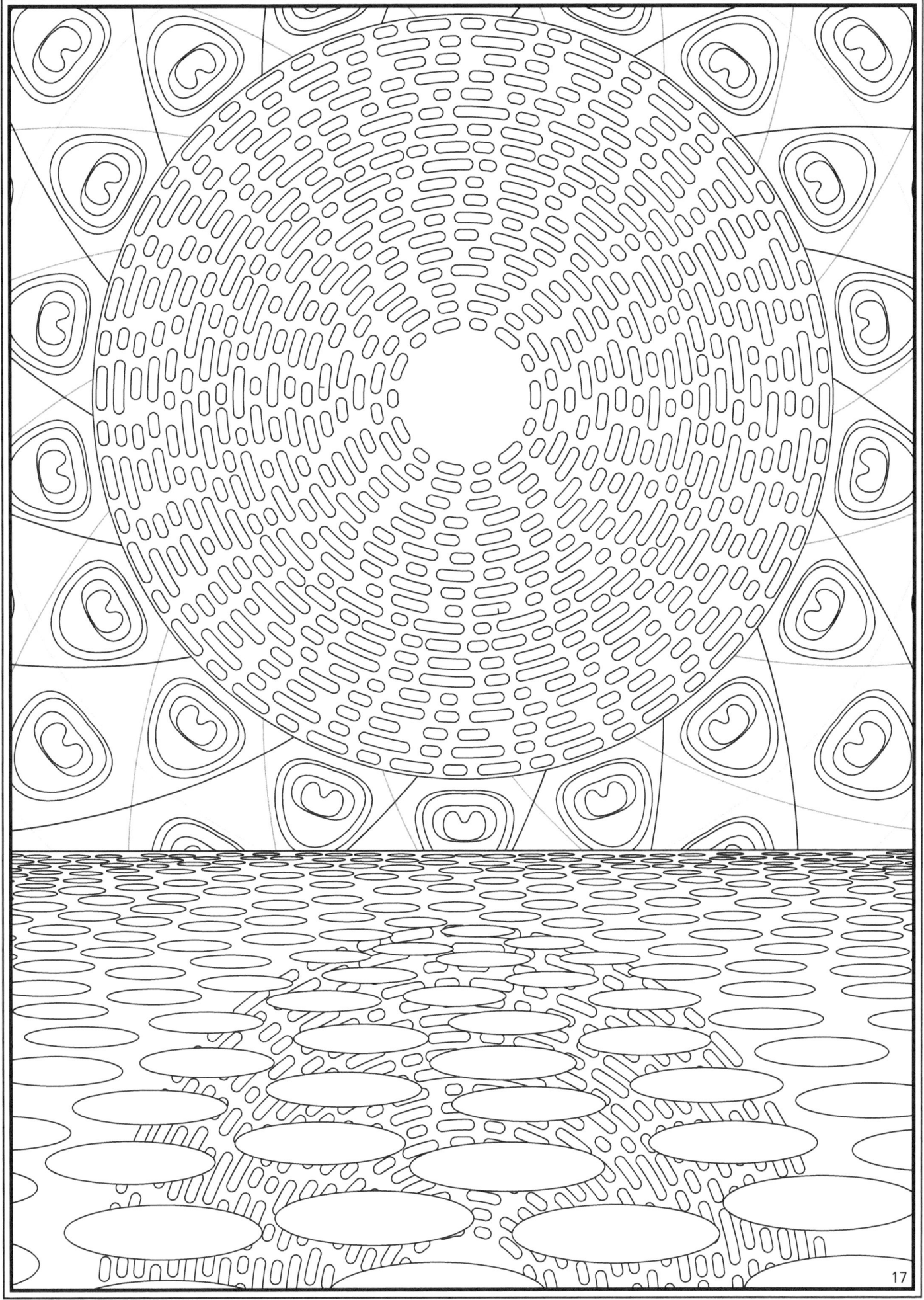

17

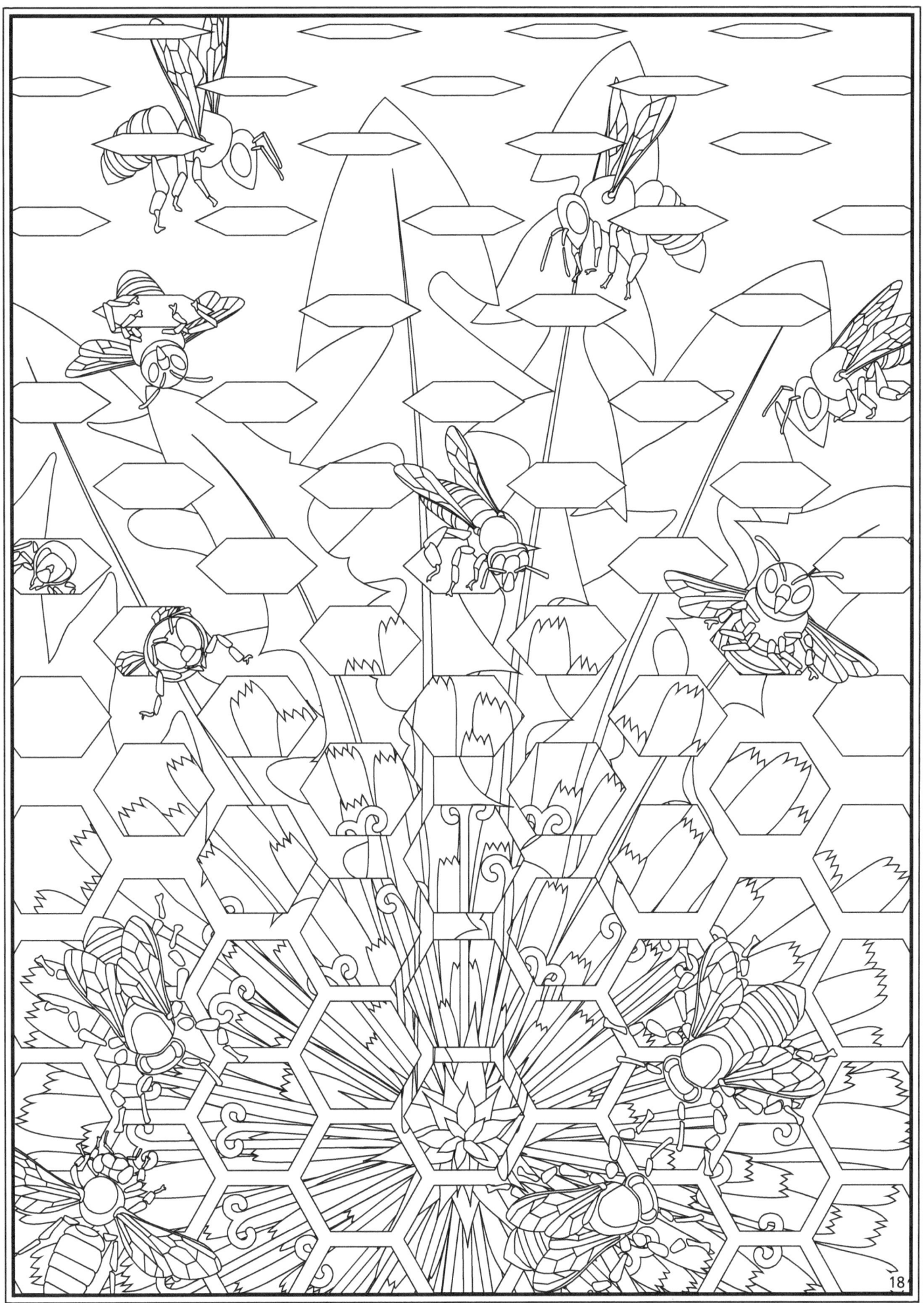

18

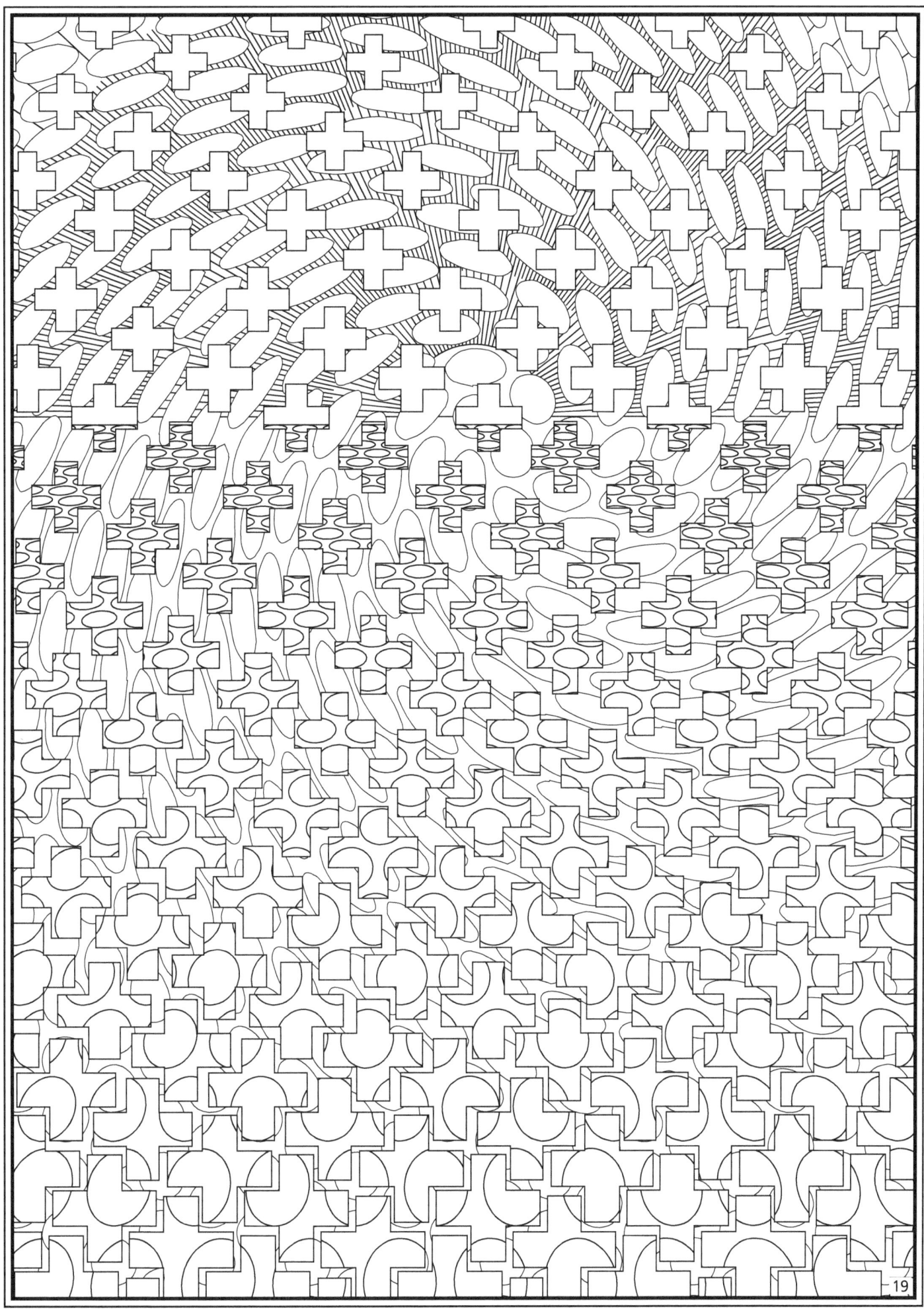

19

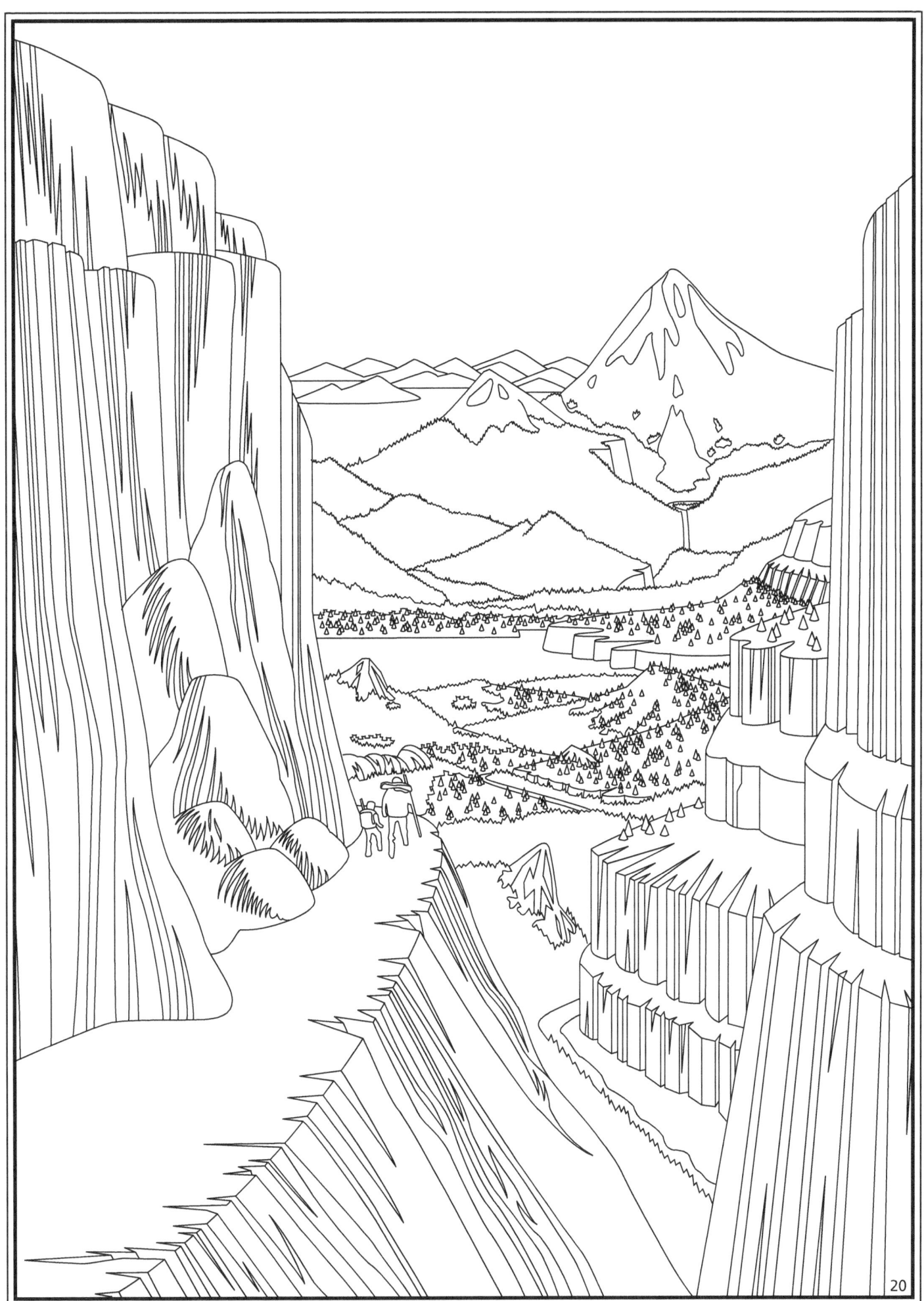

20

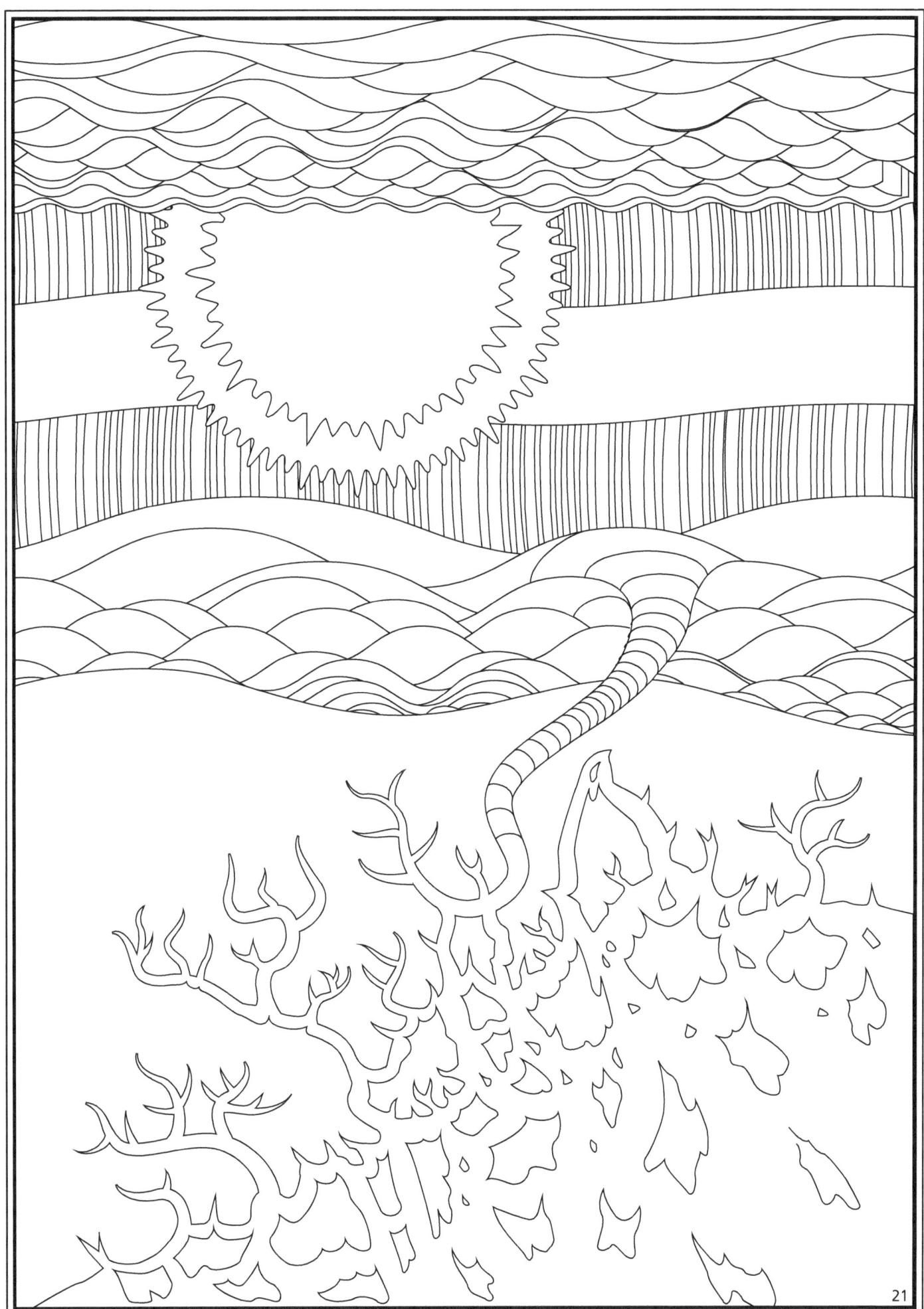

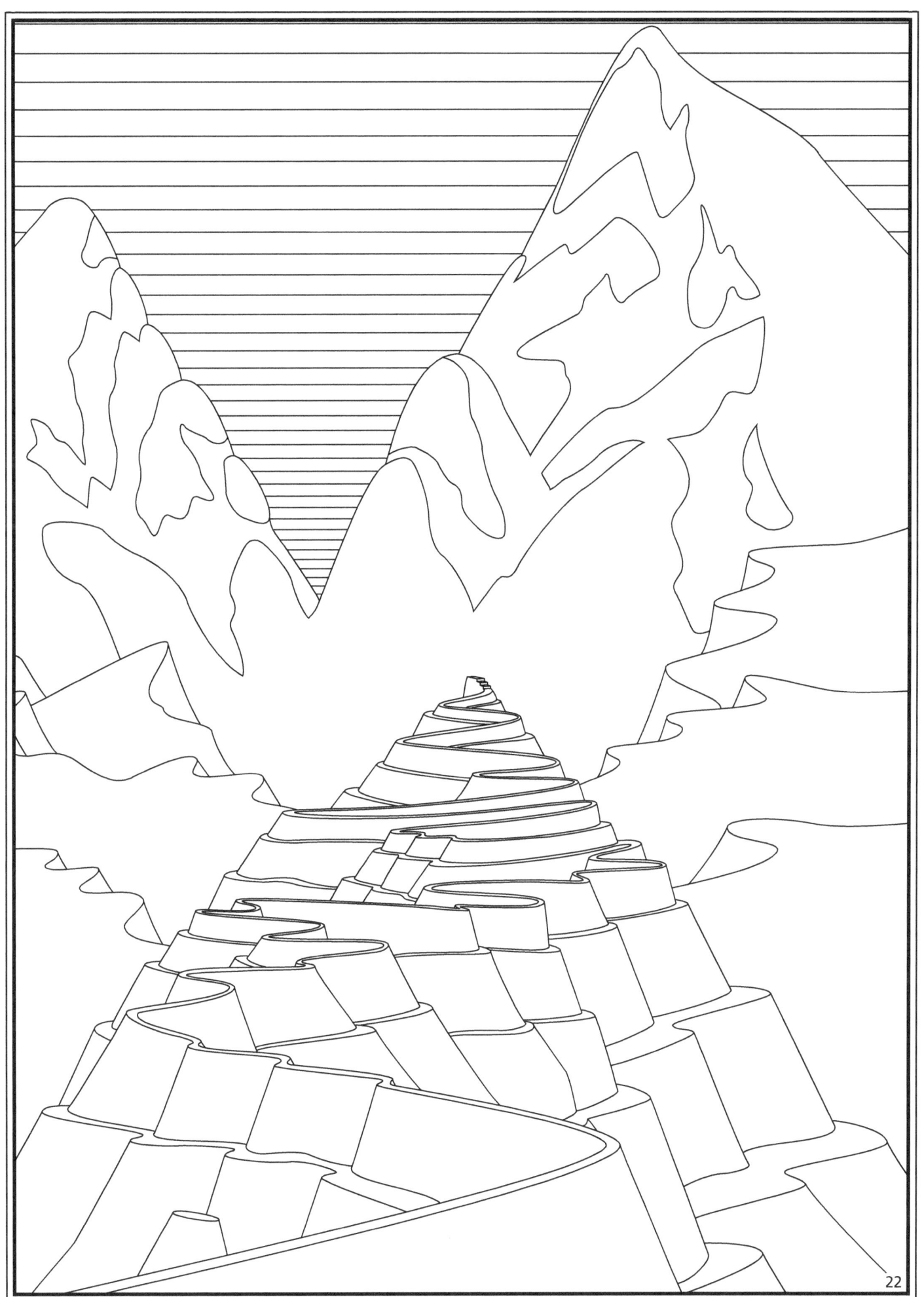

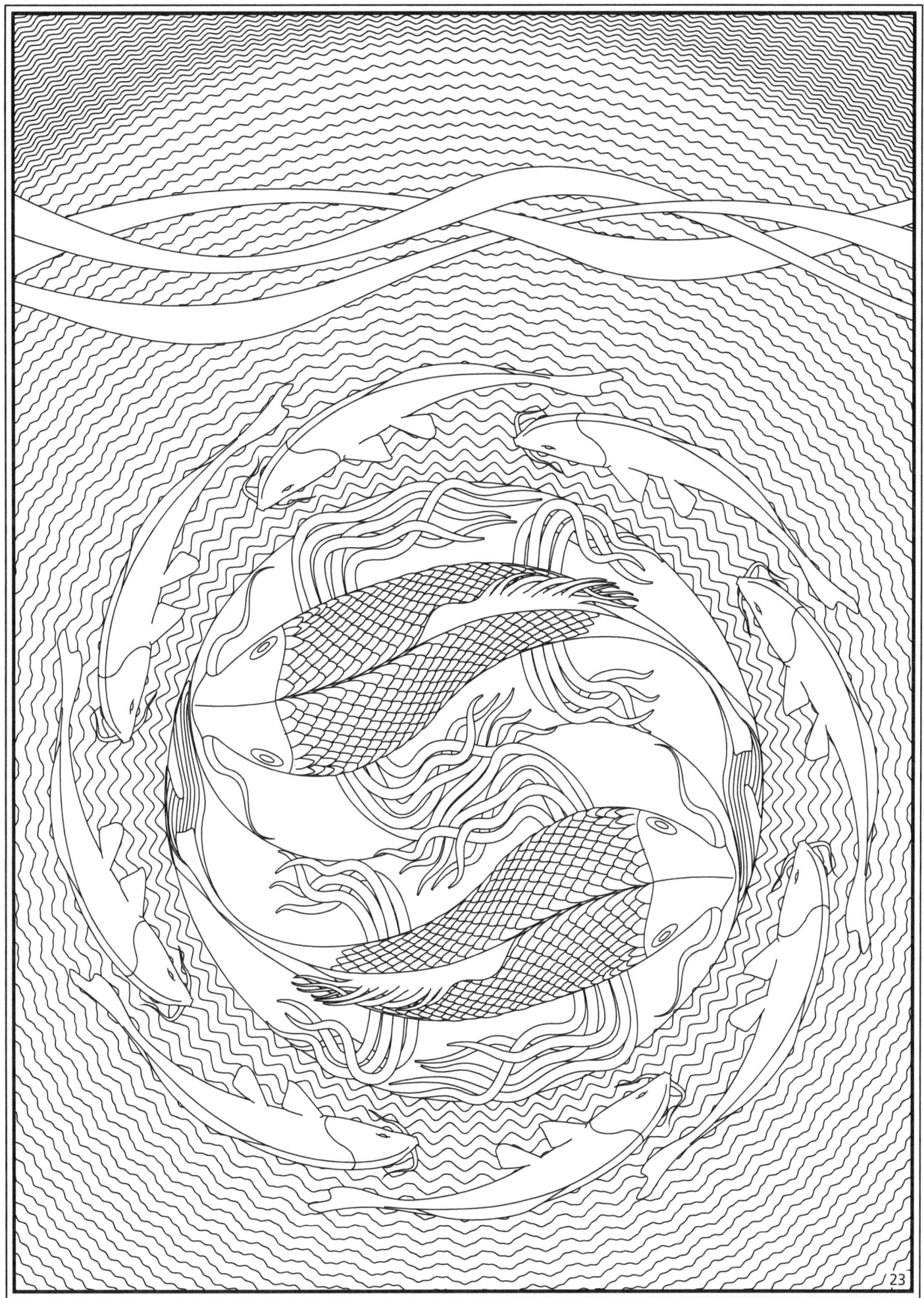

23

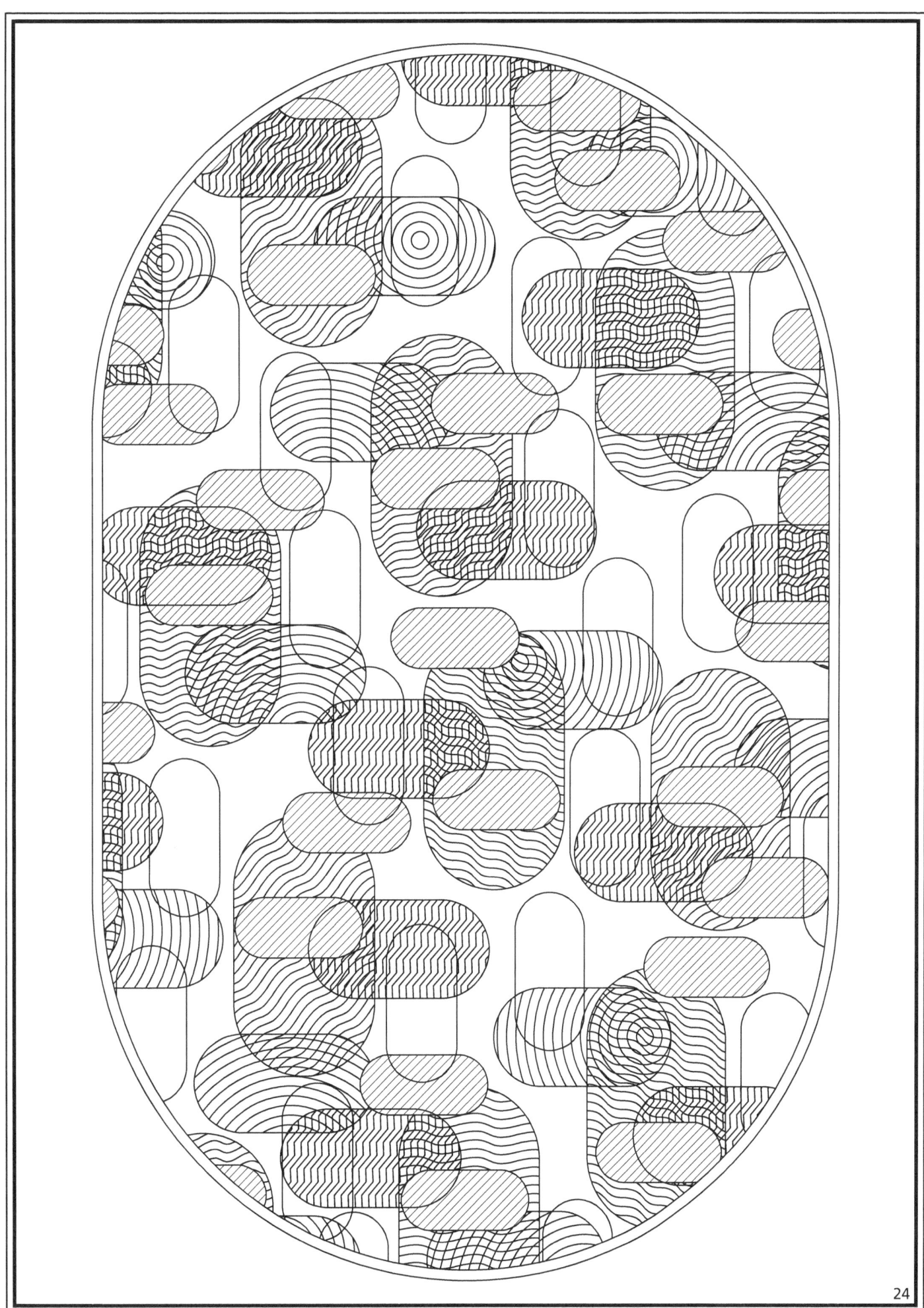

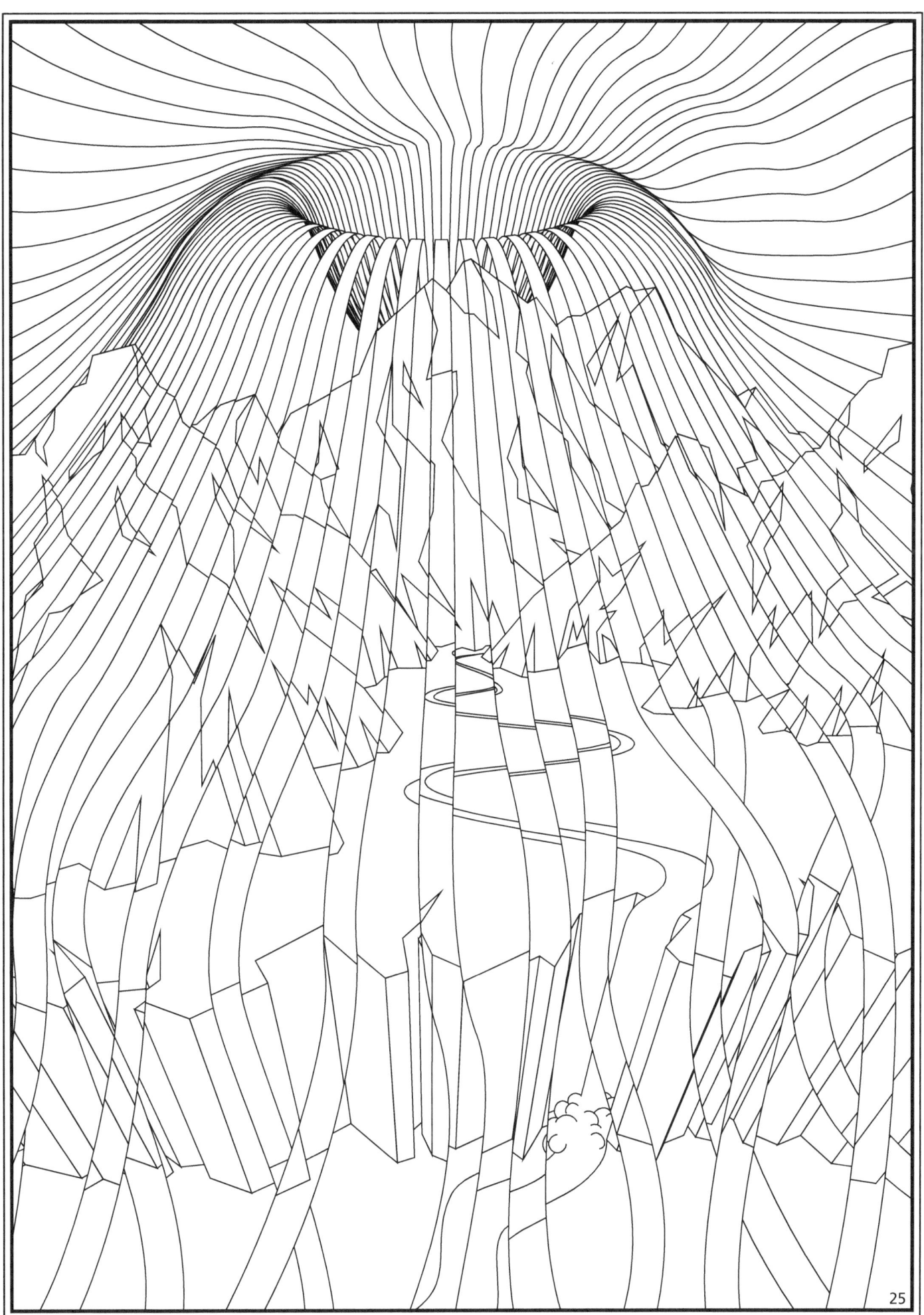

25

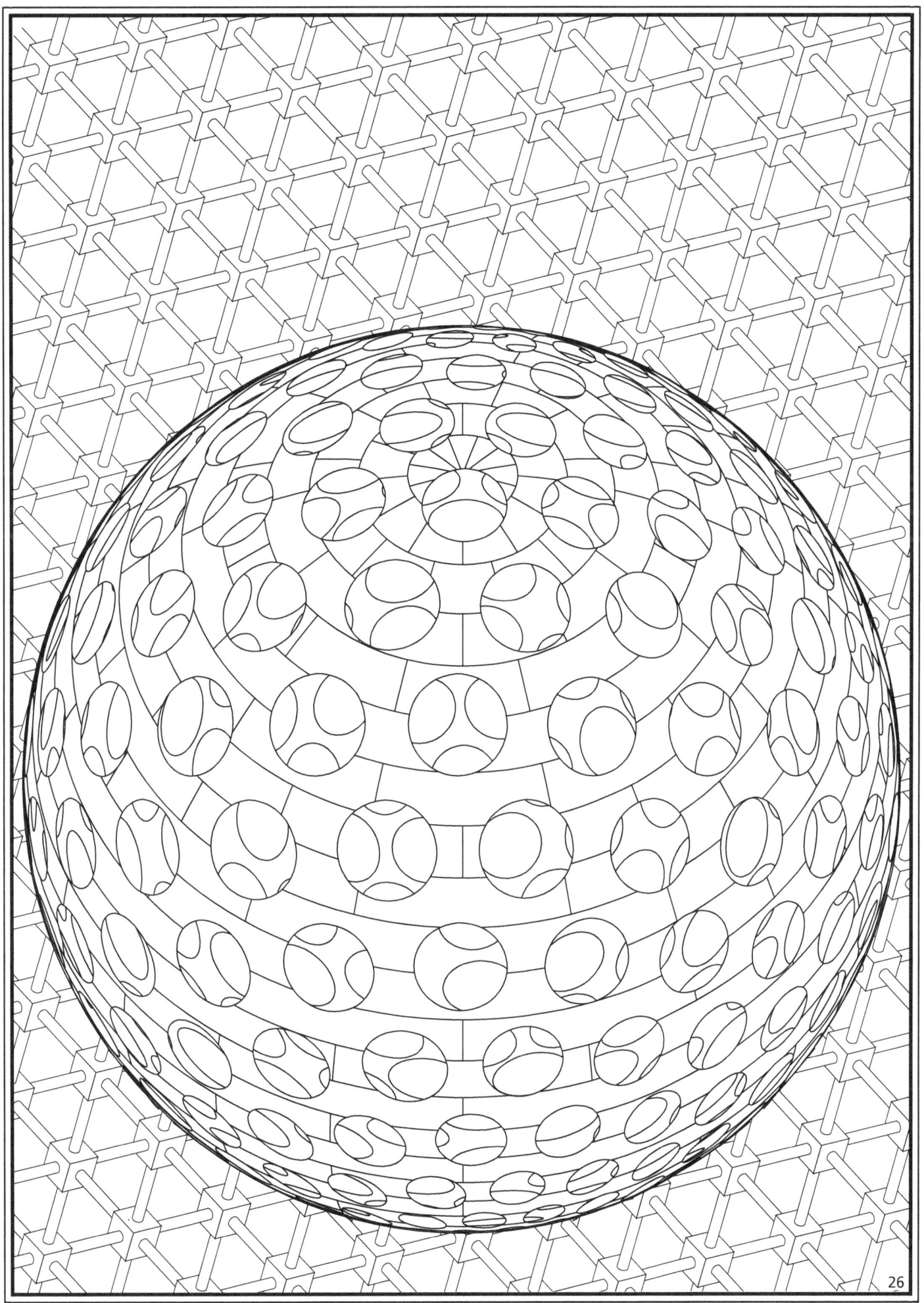

26

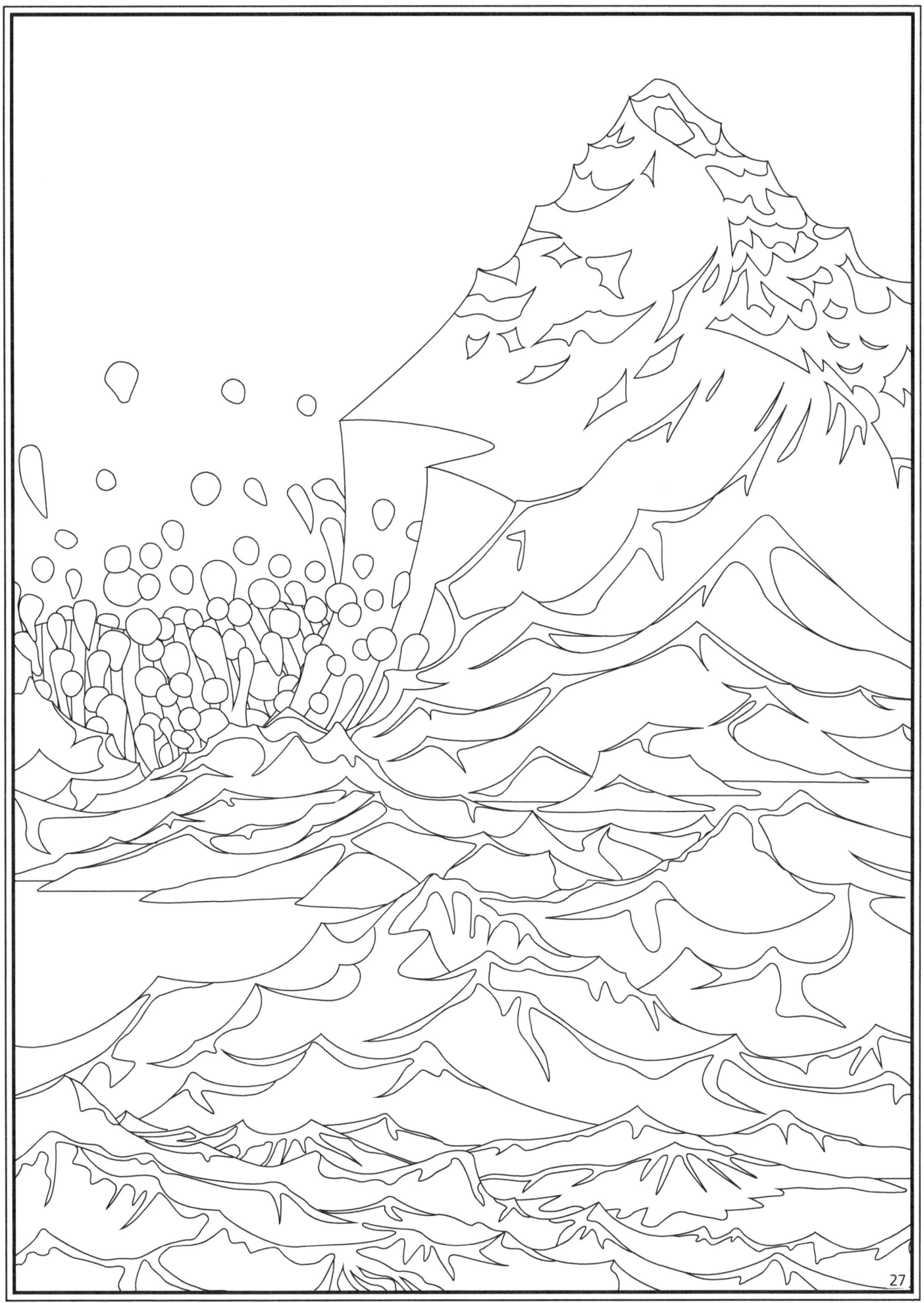

27

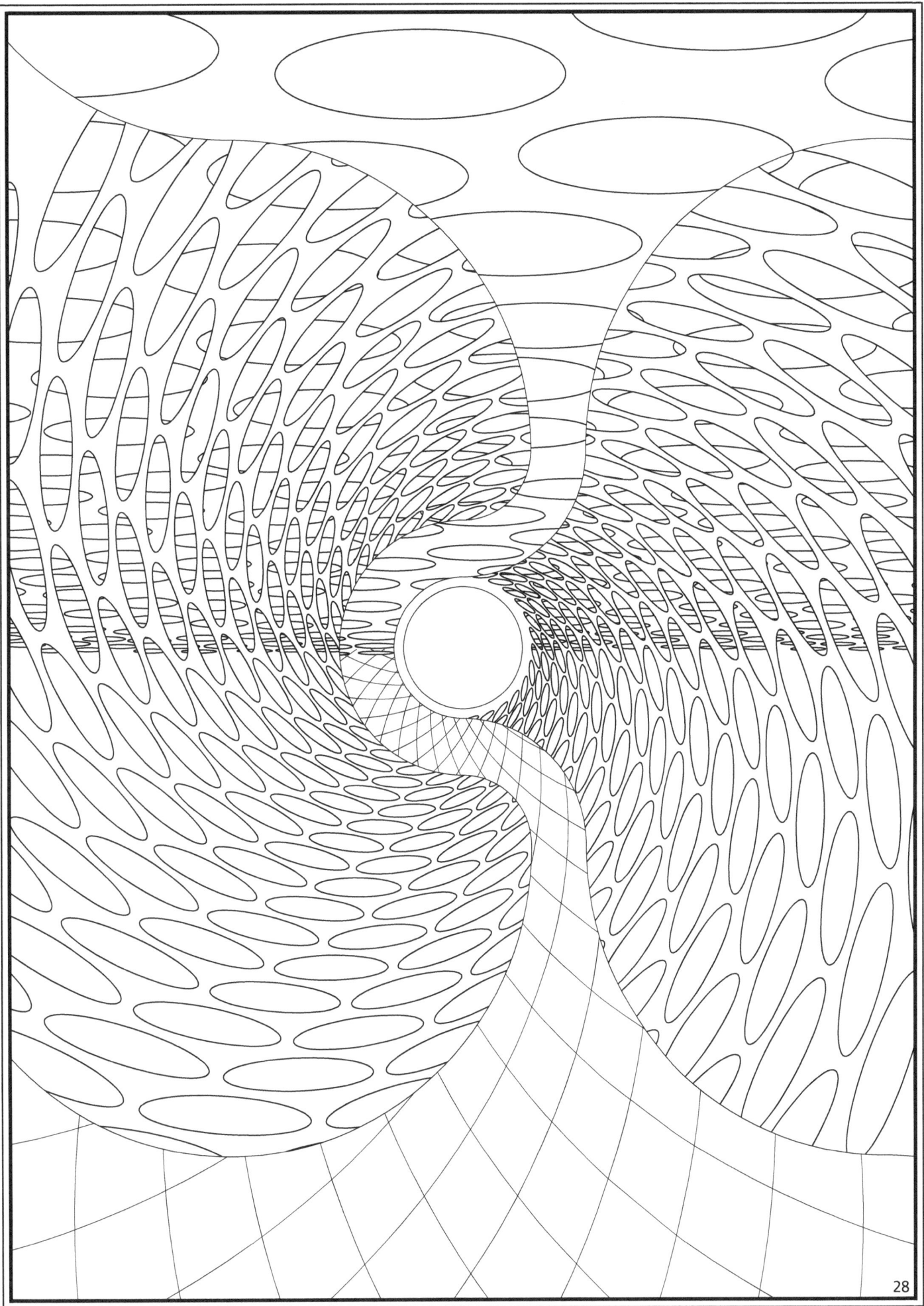

28

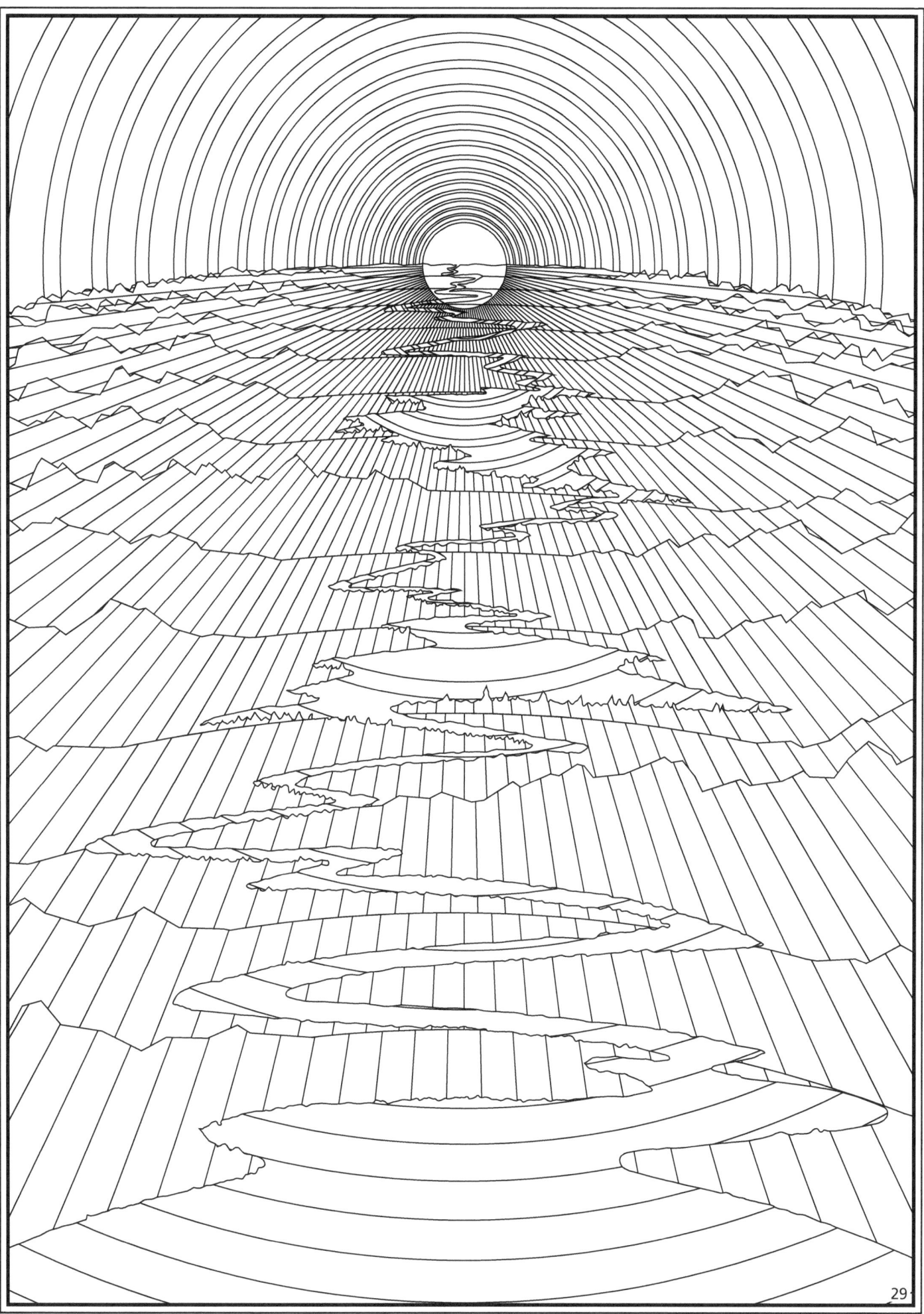

29

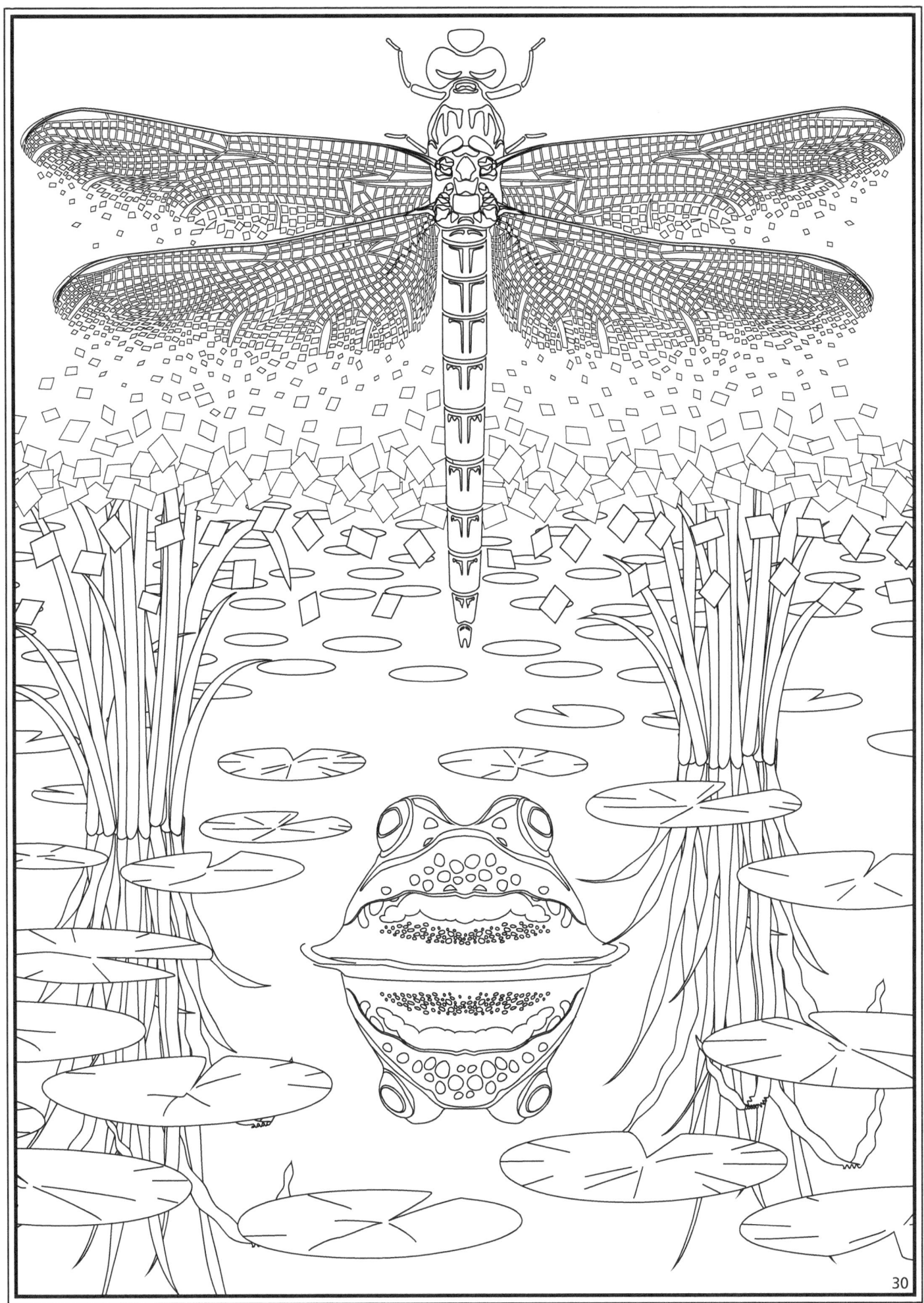

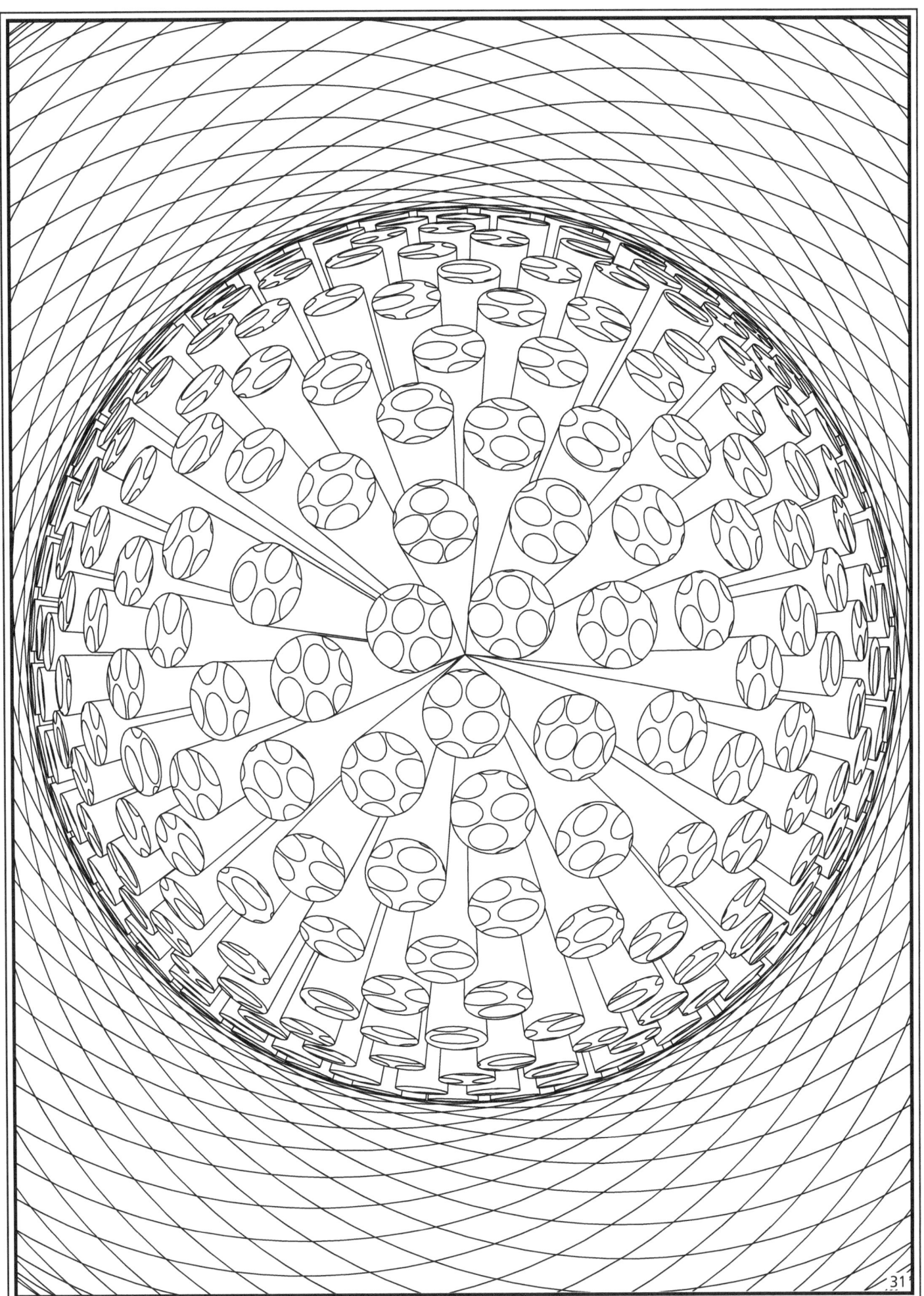

31

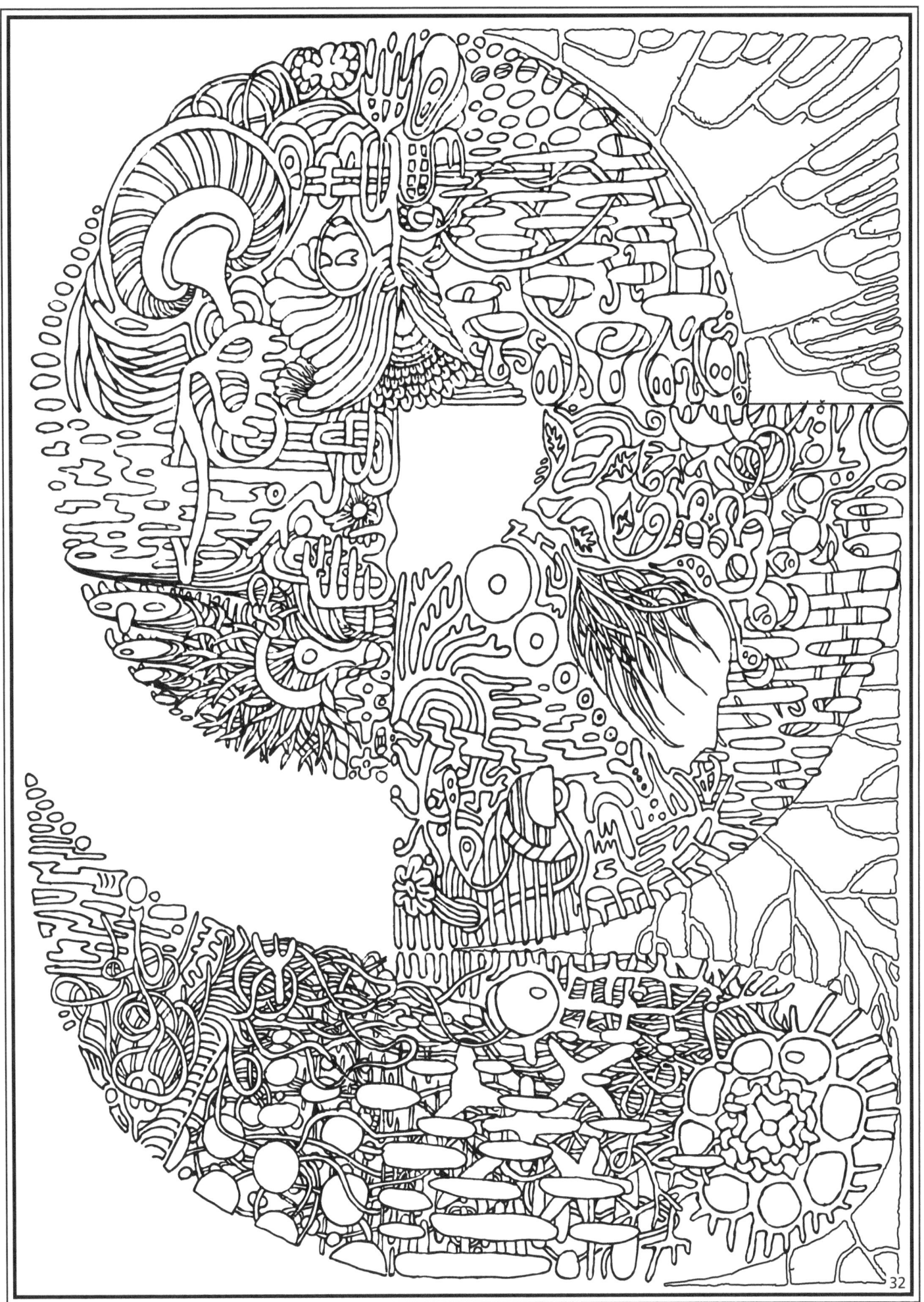